JANIELA RUSSELL

Wedding Warriors

Enlisting Your Wedding Party for Prayer Combat

First published by Noble Publishing House 2025

Copyright © 2025 by Janiela Russell

All rights reserved. No part of this publication may be reproduced, stored or transmitted in any form or by any means, electronic, mechanical, photocopying, recording, scanning, or otherwise without written permission from the publisher. It is illegal to copy this book, post it to a website, or distribute it by any other means without permission.

Janiela Russell asserts the moral right to be identified as the author of this work.

Unless otherwise noted, all scriptures are from THE HOLY BIBLE, ENGLISH STANDARD VERSION®, Copyright© 2001 by Crossway, a publishing ministry of Good News Publishers. Used by permission.

Scripture quotations marked (NKJV) are taken from the NEW KING JAMES VERSION®. Copyright© 1982 by Thomas Nelson, Inc. Used by permission. All rights reserved.

All rights reserved. This book or any portion thereof may not be reproduced or used in any manner whatsoever without the express written permission of the publisher except for the use of brief quotations in a book review.

First edition

This book was professionally typeset on Reedsy.
Find out more at reedsy.com

This book is dedicated to every person who dreams of their happily ever after. This has been a labor of love and patience from the Holy Spirit to His special child (me, it's me). He has taught me so much about preparation and relationships through this process. This book is dedicated to every marriage that has and will choose to honor God with the decision to communicate with Christ about their covenant.

Contents

Acknowledgments	iii
Introduction	1
Don't Forget To Pray!	11
More Than A Title	18
More Than A Pretty Face	22
Love	23
Joy	28
Peace	31
The Characteristics We Don't Pray For	37
Patience	37
Kindness	41
Goodness	43
The Characteristics We Neglect	46
Gentleness	46
Self-Control	49
Faithfulness	53
Let Him Read This	57
More Than a Day	64
Commitment	64
Maid/Matron of Honor	70
Best Man	72
Parents of the Bride	73
Parents of the Groom	74
Friends	76

Family	77
Church Family	78
Clergy	79
Covering the Wedding Party Prayers	81
Vision	81
Leadership	82
Glorifying God	83
Provision	83
Bride for Husband Prayer	84
Helpmeet	86
Encourager	86
Holy Standard	87
Honesty	88
Continue to Pursue	89
Baggage	89
Relationship with Christ	90
Salvation	91
Favor	91
Communication	92
Scriptures	94
About the Author	97

Acknowledgments

Jesus, you know you are that dude. All glory, praise, and honor goes to my Most High King. Thank you for charging me with this assignment and allowing the message to grow roots in me. Thank you for choosing me as your Prophet, Mouthpiece, and Oracle. These are not titles I take lightly. You are worthy of everything I am and so much more. YHWH I have no words. Selah.

Thank you to my parent's perfectly imperfect marriage for a loving foundation and picture of the process of love. I am grateful for your dedication to each other for 40+ years of faithful love. Thank you Dad for choosing Christ over and over in public and behind closed doors. Thank you for your character and tenacity to follow Christ as you lead our family. Thank you for truly loving my mother out loud. Thank you for giving life to your dreams and for giving me your face. We're not half bad-looking if you ask me.

Wedding Warriors would not be possible without the queen of submission, my beautiful mother. Thank you for your ability to love an imperfect man who decided to try again. Thank you for being comforting, calm, and hilarious. Thank you for modeling grace and creating space for me to blossom into the strong woman I am today. Thank you for your encouragement and trust. Your sweet spirit is compelling. Thank you for singing, over me, to me, and with me. Mom, you are so special and strong. Thank you for your grace, humility, and compassion for our family. For me.

To my mentor, Katrina. My world would not be the same without your wisdom, insight, and counsel. Thank you for your intercession on my behalf. Thank you for hours of conversation and encouragement. I am grateful to every friend for having my back in the way only you were designed to have it. Thank you for your spoken hope, challenge, clarifying questions, and open rebuke. I appreciate you! Thank you for every hour you've spent talking with me about Wedding Warriors from idea to today.

To my coach, Meagan! Girl, thank you! I needed every bit of what you offered me to obey God! Thank you for working with me so diligently and encouraging me that this is a message the world needs now and long after I am no longer present.

Introduction

The Uninformed Truth

I was uninformed about the actual responsibilities of being a wedding warrior. More commonly known as a bridesmaid (or a groomsman). Honestly, I never even looked at the word until now—a maid of the bride. I wasn't aware that planning a wedding would be more than physical. I did not think about the emotional drain that would arise or the spiritual support that should take place. The support needed is way more than we think, more than what most of us are taught.

When most people hear the word "wedding," they think of a white gown, flowers, and a beautifully decorated church or room filled with friends and family. We get excited and want to see the size of the diamond he was able to secure. We immediately think about the outer garments rather than the spiritual armor required. Most do not immediately see a picture of covenant, purity, the beginning of a lifelong sanctification process, or an image of Christ and the church. This is what marriage in the Bible signifies, but we seem to neglect these themes for the world's picture.

The image of Christ and the church should put most believers at attention because they are becoming more like Christ. However, we all seem to be aloof to the fact that marriage is more than a day, more than a physical chain of events. It is not always evident that the bride and groom have officially put a bull's eye on their back in the spirit realm because they are entering into a covenant. A covenant is more than a contract. It is an agreement that is sealed in a way that cannot be undone in God's eyes. There is no physical way to "take back" the agreement because the exchange between the two parties is not intended to be reversed. We are not playing UNO here.

Marriage is a covenant relationship aiming to love one another as Christ loves us. This language seems spiritual and flowery, but the enemy desires to tear down those vowing to represent Christ's love on Earth. The wedding day is, in fact, the declaration and celebration in the natural and spirit. Those who have willingly agreed to stand up at the wedding must know that they have agreed to be physically present and provide spiritual protection.

To stand up at a wedding, you need to be emotionally available, a shoulder to lean on, and a prayer partner to both parties, collectively and individually. The reason you will need to be emotionally available is the simple fact that this process will require your heart. You will need to be a safe space to talk , cry things out and pray through. Caring for others will require some level of sacrifice on your part, and if you are not ready to give that much of yourself, you may not be prepared to *serve* in this way. You will need to lend your heart to care for the bride and groom. It will be so much more than dreaming up decor and having brunch.

To be emotionally available, you'll need to be emotionally healthy enough for honest introspection. This will require self-love in an abundant way to share your overflow of care and consideration. This idea would eliminate the jealous bridesmaid as you enter the process with the heart of a servant and the knowledge that you are strengthening this brick in the Kingdom of Heaven. We can often get jealous of others, but we are fighting ourselves when we remain jealous of our brothers and sisters in Christ! It is counterintuitive to fight something that is building you up. We have to see marriage as a covenant to understand that the Kingdom is getting stronger. We need to strengthen the family dynamic, but it starts with two.

INTRODUCTION

Knowing that the wedding day is an outward profession of two people entering into a covenant and becoming one as Christ does with the church is **half the battle**. But you have to know that it is a battle. When you watch movies where there is a competition of sorts whether it be dance or sports one of the things the enemy does is steal moves. The opponents are not creative enough to choreograph or run plays they've planned on their own. Instead, they spy and plot on the opposing team to replicate their greatness and win. The teams quickly learn not to trust the opposite camps nor underestimate them.

Although the team we usually root for is more talented, creative, and honest, they take a hit that they could have been prepared for. If high school students can be shrewd enough to do this, how much more would your adversary? This is a very basic example of what the enemy does. His aim is to pervert (twist) the representation of who Christ and His bride, the church, are. This is quite literally wickedness. Wickedness is not always this big scary thing; it can be a slight variation from what the Lord desires, twisting the truth ever so slightly. Humanity took on old Satan's job (worship) because he tried to take the glory of God for himself.

If we know that the enemy aims to distort and destroy humanity's view of God, we should expect that he will do all he can to war against God's ambassadors on Earth. Once we accept Jesus as Lord of our life we are given the ministry of reconciliation as we have been reconciled to God. Sin separated us and Jesus provided a way back to the Father. Marriage is the exact representation of Christ and His bride, the church. We cannot continue to be naive or neglect the all-out assault of the enemy by being unprepared. Let's not be silent against the schemes of the enemy by pretending he's not there. We can thwart his plans by taking some intentional steps.

The wedding day is much like a baptism. Baptism is the outward confession of an inward decision of your covenant with Christ. We experience baptisms in the community, whether it is one person, ten, or 10,000. Much like the preparation for a baptism, we should truly understand the public proclamation of our natural marriage. I remember way back in the day before people walked around with gadgets in their pockets. Before YouTube, can you imagine? I decided to go public with my faith and get baptized. I was at the ripe old age of four and I still remember sitting in our youth building with my Children's Pastor. I remember him asking me if I knew what being 'saved' and getting baptized meant. So I stated that I did and continue to grow in revelation of all that baptism signifies.

Many Christians have already decided to follow Christ before they decide to get water baptized. The decision is fixed, but you are bringing it to your community to celebrate, make a statement, and gain encouragement through accountability. In addition to baptisms, two distinct experiences stand out as a demarcation of my relationship with Christ. The first was while working, I would often take naps on my break, and my alarm was a song that quoted Psalm 96. Please go read it aloud. It makes this whole experience even more specific. It's okay to laugh, I did eventually.

While grabbing a snack and returning to work, I left my phone at my desk. I had only snoozed my alarm, not turned it off. While I was out of the room, the entire song played. When I returned to my desk, I was informed of what happened. Part of me was embarrassed because one of the song lyrics states, "all the gods of the others are worthless idols." Very true, but not exactly what I wanted the entire office to hear. When settling back into work, I heard the LORD whisper; *they'll know you're mine*. I took pride at that moment because the Lord chose to claim me before man. So I'll continue to claim Him before men. (Matthew 10:32-33)

The second and more recent experience like this started in my parent's living room near the beginning of the pandemic. I know it's a bad word, but we made it. I was watching my church online, and that Sunday, the Pastor decided we would worship in song for the entire service. I began to pace the room in a very specific pattern which I realized was an infinity or figure eight. The infinity sign is the symbol of covenant. In that intimate space, the LORD told me, He made a new covenant with me. I was like, cool, that's pretty dope, God. I also said that would be a cool tattoo. I periodically thought about that moment and even the tattoo at times, but it was not at the forefront of my mind. Then, summer of 2021, the Lord spoke to me and asked if I was going to get that tattoo. My response was sure I wasn't aware that it was a requirement. Within a day or so, He replied by saying, it's like I proposed to you, but you never put the ring on. He wanted to mark that moment with me with a symbol.

At that moment, I knew I had to go public by marking the moment. I had to build the altar. I knew this mark couldn't be too small or hidden as it is a sign of the covenant with the Lord or as His name is printed YHWH made with me. So it now sits on the outside of my forearm, about four inches wide. I look tougher than I am, for sure, but much like a baptism at the moment, I wear the agreement of my devotion to Him and His to me on my skin. I love this story and the fact that my tattoo artist is a believer who got to witness this *stamp* of the covenant.

This bit of ink on my arm is a symbol, a statement of the fact that I am in covenant with Christ. This means that I am quite literally marked with the name of the Most High God. I cannot erase it. I welcome the accountability that challenges any behavior contrary to the sign of my covenant.

If the Lord is this serious about going public to mark a moment with me, imagine how much the covenant of marriage means to Him. The Lord was serious about these instances being a part of my journey of a growing personal relationship with Him. So a wedding is more than just a party. It is the marking of a covenant, not only between two people but between a man, his wife, and **their** God.

Some years ago, I stood up as a bridesmaid for a young lady I knew through church. I was surprised and excited to be a part of the couple's union. The bride-to-be took a few ladies out to lunch, where we were formally asked to be her bridesmaids and given gifts for our participation. This meeting happened about a year before the set wedding date. This was the first non-family wedding I was requested to participate in. I said yes, but yes, to what? I felt honored that someone would ask me to stand up at their wedding because it is such a huge landmark in their life. I was surprised to be chosen because we were not close, but I believe I was selected because of my faith and personality.

At that time, the bride-to-be saw me serving our young adult ministry and just being genuine with others. All that said, I did not know what standing up at someone's wedding required, so I searched the internet for some answers. I (#teambride) was responsible for planning the shower, bachelorette party, and the wedding itself.

Therefore, I needed to make myself available for fittings, decorating, setup, teardown, and other preparations. I also looked to see if any apps would help in the planning (There are tons!).

As a young—emphasis on young—woman of God, it did not even cross my mind that there was a spiritual preparation that I needed to research and provide to the bride. I just thought it meant I would help out in planning and celebrating. The spiritual preparation was not apparent to me because it was not something I was ever taught. No one sits little girls down while playing dress up to show them that part of marriage.

We imitate weddings and being a mother without the knowledge that there is or there should be a spiritual attachment to these events. For example, a five-year-old girl might know a man finds you, you like him, eventually when you are old enough and have your ducks in a row (to each his own standard), a ring comes, a knee is bent, a day when you feel like a princess occurs, and then you live happily ever after.

As girls, we might play out a whole ceremony in our heads. We know the roles, but there is nothing beyond the natural. No one taught me that you should pray before a wedding, let alone a marriage. I was taught that you would need to work to *maintain* a marriage and that you would need to pray to get through tough times. However, I was not taught that you could get a headstart proactively praying beforehand. We encourage young women to pray for their mate, but not for the life that comes after their wedding day.

For generations, Christians have neglected to teach our little ones to pray in preparation for one of the biggest decisions of their lives.

We teach girls that sitting a certain way or to roughhouse is not proper. We teach them not to speak a certain way, not to belch. We teach them how to apply makeup and to dress appropriately for different occasions and environments, but not how to cover themselves and their future in prayer. Of course, prayer is important in every aspect of life, but every aspect of life is not equally attacked. Marriage is on the enemy's radar more because it is such a powerful representation of Christ's love for the church.

In a group of three bridesmaids, I would have expected someone to remember to cover the marriage in prayer or that there should be some type of spiritual preparation other than mentioning Jesus during mani-pedi appointments. We met several times about wardrobe and other specifics but not about the bride and groom's spiritual future. I believe we would have jumped at the chance to cover the bride and groom this way, but it's not really something we were taught. The even crazier thing is we had a culture of prayer at the church we all attended together. It is not that we were 'bad Christians' we just didn't know to use the tool of prayer for the project of marriage before there was ever a problem to be solved.

Typically the most spiritual preparation has been marriage counseling. However, the experience of this wedding and countless conversations have led me to the conclusion that counseling should not be the sum of your spiritual preparation. Also, there is nothing wrong with having Pastoral Counseling and a licensed counselor because, if we're being honest, we need all the tools we can get!

Unfortunately, the culture of the American church has not exemplified spiritual preparation. Therefore, we have not claimed it as a priority. Let me be crystal clear, marriage counseling is a MUST, but it's not the totality of your spiritual preparation. It would be like attending church and never opening your Bible to read it for yourself. You have a relationship with other believers and are exposed to the preacher's perspective. Still, you do not engage in the very thing the LORD has offered you, a personal relationship with Him. By doing this, we prioritize results over the procedure. For example, we prioritize purity but do not necessarily provide steps to stay pure. We tell young men and women (like they are the only ones struggling with purity) to wait but do not give healthy habits to combat an oversexualized society.

As a body of believers, we have not educated ourselves or the following generations of the value of purity. We are told not to have premarital sex pretending that is the only thing that defiles our souls. The church has not shared why living according to God's principles is and will be a blessing to you and your future. We need to address the why not the what so people have a true understanding of their choice to wait or not. For years the conversation has been don't do *it*, and many try to obey an empty rule without understanding which has not presented great results. Blindly reaching for a goal is aimless because there is no resolve. The goal does not mean much when it is not personal or worth any value. A goal without its purpose will not be obtained.

If the goal is a healthy, thriving marriage, I am urging that prayer is a huge step in the preparation to obtain it. However, we don't want to just maintain marriages. Instead, we want to cultivate marriages that are thriving, healthy, and grow healthier.

Imagine if our cars had no safety testing before they came to market?

Would you feel safe knowing they did not test anything after putting it together, hoping the "normal" car maintenance would keep you safe? There is a procedure and process that helps us to be more certain we are prepared for our journey. Why wouldn't we seek God's process for His establishment? There is much more preparation than purity for a successful marriage. The Bible speaks about a husband giving himself up for his wife as Christ gave of Himself. This beautiful language encourages husbands to sacrifice their will to love as Christ did. Christ loved us so much that He gave His life in exchange. You do not 'arrive' at that level of love without the understanding that your life is poured out and to be lived as your life is not your own. We are not born with the innate desire to give our lives like Christ. That is something He develops in us until we meet Him in glory.

I am currently serving as a bridesmaid again, and I cannot tell you that I have been perfect in praying for the engaged couple every day, but I have prayed weekly. Being intentional about covering their relationship in prayer gives me joy and hope that they will not just have a marriage but one that has been brought before the Lord. A marriage surrendered before the throne of God. A marriage that is life-giving, pure, and the representation of Christ and His bride, the church on Earth.

How is it that the longest-married couples in the church 'survive' marriage? Even as I write that line, I find it daunting the ideas that I still have rooted in my thinking. Christians literally have the handbook on marriage, but we still need to take the practical tools to excel in a lifelong marriage full of joy. No, you will not always be happy, but you can choose to have joy. You can study for the test and put it in God's hands before entering into a covenant. I've watched my parents, who are far from perfect, become each other's favorite people the longer I have lived. They wake up and actively choose each other. This did not just occur. It came from them planting seeds of unity and devotion to one another for over forty years.

Back to the original bridal party - We went through the process of picking and trying on dresses and accessories, planning the bridal shower, choosing the flowers, and scheduling the rehearsal dinner. We even met just as bridesmaids to discuss other things concerning the wedding. We planned the bachelorette party/event and shopped for all the little decorations and gifts that were important to the big day. Unfortunately, it wasn't until after hair, makeup, and nail appointments had been completed. Not until after we were all dressed and at the venue, not until after guests were arriving and the rose petals were spread over the entrance, that I realized we planned a day that would start the rest of their lives together without including God.

No, I don't mean a judge was officiating the ceremony or that they hadn't gone to marriage counseling through our local church. I meant that as a friend, I had not put any effort into praying for their lifelong covenant other than blessing our meals. I did not pray for their strength or that the Lord would fill them with His joy, peace, and wisdom. I did not ask the Lord to give them increase and health. I did not ask that the Lord draw them closer to Himself and each other. They were and still are equally yoked. Both the bride and groom were active volunteering members of our church, but we hadn't included Christ as a major, if not the most important factor in their union as their support system.

Of course, when I realized, I asked for us to gather just moments before walking out, and I tried to pray Heaven down. I instantly knew that I could have been doing this the entire wedding journey. This was my feeble attempt to fix my oversight. I should have been praying Heaven down for the last six months to a year. I felt like I did them a disservice because I was there in the natural, but I should have used the best asset I have, the power of prayer. For this oversight, I have repented.

Don't Forget To Pray!

Why is forgetting to pray such a big deal?

The enemy attacks the sanctity of marriage because it is, in fact, the exact representation of Christ and the church to the world. Therefore, being on guard is not just smart; it's necessary. In mainstream American culture, marriage has become about a ring, the biggest party of your life, and social status. We've neglected to see marriage as a covenant that invites the enemy's disdain and his fallen purpose to kill, steal, and destroy. (John 10:10) Marriage is the very foundation of the family. For some, the beginning of their spiritual heritage. Understanding the true weight of the marriage covenant will truly allow us to enter in with a sober mind. We cannot just assume that marriage life ends happily ever after as the movies show us.

One of the most beautiful things we can do as believers is to choose a marriage partner with a spiritual legacy in mind. Why? Because your ceiling is their foundation. Your children get to grow from your very highest height. If your desire is not to bear biological children, you get to bear children in the spirit. Your commitment to Christ is passed along to the local church and community you all participate in. People get to see you operating as parts of the Godhead throughout your relationship, covering and submitting to one another. It is a beautiful dance and display of God's love and sanctification of man.

For instance, my parents were raised in extremely different households emphasizing religion, not relationships. My Father's parents believed in the Lord. However, it was exemplified through sending him to a private Christian school where he learned the mechanics of the religion, not necessarily how to develop a personal relationship with Christ. My Father came into a relationship with Christ in his twenties.

On the other hand, my mother grew up in a house where her Father was a Minister. She had a family who was always in church, but she gained her relationship with Christ through music at a young age. Her mother and siblings would travel from city to city in Alabama, ministering through song. It is essential to realize that even though their family foundation was different, they came together to create something new. The spiritual heritage I was born into directly resulted from their union. Both my parents had faithfully served in our local church since before I was born, and they created a God-centered home life.

My home life was not perfect by any means, but I grew up in a household where we learned to depend on God for everything. We would often read Psalm 34 and stand on the expressed promises of God. We learned to engage daily in the Word and prayer with my parents. They modeled their relationship with the Father as a couple and continued to guide my siblings and me in the same pursuit. I witnessed my parents pray daily together before they invited anyone else into that space. We did not always understand, but we knew it was sacred. They were laying the foundation of their relationship with Christ before their fruit.

In my experience, those who are prepared to the best of their ability have an easier time pivoting when things need to be adjusted. Preparation helps condition your mind, body, and spirit to respond appropriately. For example, if you hit an obstacle in your wedding planning or relationship and you have conditioned yourself and your crew to speak biblically instead of allowing the world's principles to influence your decisions, there would be greater success. Overcoming obstacles with healthy, biblical principles will be easier and quicker. For example, you didn't see an illness coming in the first two years of your marriage, but you and your spouse have cultivated a culture of prayer not only between the two of you but also with your community. It becomes second nature to run to God. When you can immediately go to the One who works all things out for your good instead of wondering why this is happening to you? When your heart is settled in the promises that you have been rehearsing over one another about your health and future. You will worry less or not at all. The fear and anxiety are quieted by the roar of the peace of the living God! Your ability to be anchored in that season is much more weighty than you would be if you have surface relationships or a variety of belief systems.

We prepare for the wedding day in many ways, but we think a prayer instead of a prayer life/prayer culture will suffice. We are all aware that marriage can be difficult. You are merging two lives, identities, personalities, habits, thoughts, experiences, possible traumas, and memories into one. Marriage is more than the two becoming one flesh. Even in the area of two becoming one flesh, the potential spiritual baggage of the flesh is still glaring on your wedding night. We can proactively remove those soul ties. We can remove perverse habits. We can call on the holiness of our Savior to bring us to a place where our spouse is not struggling with Bobby or Jamal from the seventh grade. We can allow the LORD to reset and recalibrate our bodies to Heaven's divine settings. To be touched and to desire your spouse above all others. You can safeguard your marriage relationship *before* and after you enter it.

If we are being honest, prayer is not this magical thing that changes your situation, although it can! Prayer is running to the Creator, saying I cannot handle this. I know that you love me. What do I do? Please help me to have a posture of trust and faith. Prayer is sitting and listening intently for a strategy on how to raise your family, love your spouse, and see them the way the Lord sees them.

The communication between you and your Heavenly Father is one of the most intimate ways God allows us into His space to see how much we are loved, chosen, and valued by the Lord. Christians can often forget that God wants us to have a relationship with Him. This is often stated but needs to be personalized. Prayer is one way we intentionally bring Him into our lives. We get to ward off the temptation to idolize the marriage relationship when prayer becomes the foundation of the connection between you and your spouse and those surrounding the wedding day. The habits and way we start a thing will often predict how we will continue to cultivate. If the wedding process is soaked in powerful, intentional moments of prayer, what do you think will happen in your marriage? Wouldn't it be easier to strike before you incur an injury?

Prayer shifts our perspective from our desires to Kingdom desires. We are to live as living epistles (books/testimonies) to the glory of God. So when we prioritize prayer in relationships that could otherwise consume us, we allow Heaven to speak a stronger or better word than our vision and the influence of culture.

We want to be proactive instead of reactionary because that is the Kingdom of heaven. Scripture says that Jesus, the Lamb who was slain, was slain before the foundation of the earth. This does not sound reactionary to me. Before mankind required redemption the Lord provided the way to be redeemed. Jesus won the victory over death, hell and the grave and empowers us to have victory when it comes to marriage. The world might say that it is virtually impossible to live a long, prosperous, joyful marriage, but I am convinced it is possible if we live by the principles of the Word of God. We can have victory.

There will be specific challenges each couple brings to the table and specific challenges that arise, but we have Holy Spirit to guide us through prayer concerning what to pray for in these circumstances. Holy Spirit gives us guidance and comfort and Jesus gives us the POWER to walk out the principles of the kingdom.

"Truly, truly, I say to you, whoever believes in me will also do the works that I do; and greater works than these will he do because I am going to the Father." (John 14:12, ESV)

Jesus empowers us to live a holy life. We are empowered to live and die to selfish, fleshy desires, walking in the Fruit of the Spirit. We see the uniqueness and unity in perfect harmony with the Trinity. Each person of the Trinity has His own function, but they work together to fulfill the Kingdom's purpose.

Marriage is also the platform on which the world can see selfless love. I must be the first to admit this is not a quality exemplified as much as it should be within the body of Christ. However, this is one of the relationships where we truly die to ourselves by honoring one another. You and your spouse get to show the power of love: to sacrifice for one another and show those around you true trust, love, and intimacy.

Knowing that this platform of selfless love is in view of a lost and dying world seeking hope should bring some weight and gravity to your decision. Not for the sake of people praising you because you got married but as a display of the glory of God. Your marriage can and, dare I say, should be a witness. Some of this weight gets destroyed when we trivialize marriage as a means to an end, a business deal, or a license to have sex. We cheapen the covenant when we walk through it without spiritual preparation. It is a spiritual experience. Let's give it the respect it deserves.

Many women have selected their bridesmaids as women who have been great friends in certain seasons instead of those friends who are strong in faith and fervent for Christ. From a young age, many ladies have dreams about their weddings. We tend to plan every detail, including those friends who are closest at the moment. While this makes logical sense, it does not give much room for friendships that change or grow apart. Friendships grow apart for several reasons. Friendships do not always grow up. Some of the most important reasons friendships grow apart are those that divide because of beliefs. Not to say we cut off all ties with people who do not believe the way we do, but they may not be the best people to stand with you at this moment.

Let's say you've been "besties" with a young woman throughout grade school. You might even go to church or volunteer together. And then college hits. You promise that you will keep in touch and that no matter what, this friend will be the first you call on for every life event.

You both get busy and keep in touch, but the core of your relationship is based on who you were ten years ago. You still know her favorite color and what she likes to do in her spare time, but you are not sure what her dreams are anymore. You are unaware that she has taken up a "new spiritual journey" and has different beliefs than when you were close. This is not to say that you throw away every relationship with some distance, but I am urging you to be more mindful that sometimes people change and grow in different directions.

The reasons are numerous, but one of the things of utmost importance is that your spiritual lives (and, for the purposes of this book, your faith in Christ) are equally yoked, solid, and growing. I said growing because as you grow, you want a community that is growing ahead, with, and after you. This is extremely important as we walk in discipleship. You need those who are ahead of you, those who are right with you, and those who are behind you so that you function in all three relationships. Follower. Co-Lead. Leader.

This may seem selective. To be honest, it is. If you know the Lord and have accepted Him as your Lord and Savior, who would you call on when you need help or guidance? Would you call on your friend who never stopped partying or the one who is still trying to find herself? Would you call on the friend who believes everything can be explained through logic and science, or do you call on the one who will encourage you with the Word of God? Do you call on the one who has an active prayer life and lives out the Word as she walks through life?

Do not misunderstand me when I say I prefer one over the other because we should all have people in our sphere of influence who are different from ourselves and those who do not have it all together.

Those relationships are where we are supposed to pour life, love, and grace into, not glean wisdom. We cannot expect more from a person than they can offer at a certain point. No matter how much you love the person, you cannot drink from an empty well.

I don't know about you, but I do not want to go into a fight unarmed and untrained. I definitely don't want to bring a friend who has no clue how to fight, to a battle with me. It's like walking up to the high school bully with the fragile girl who draws rainbows and unicorns in class all day (not exactly my first choice). I would want someone tough, someone who is known for winning physical altercations. I want somebody who knows they can fight and is accustomed to winning. Believe it or not, you can see the fruit of a person's life when they are winning spiritual battles. No, their life may not look perfect, but they have peace, joy, patience, etc. when logically, they should not. We need to PRAY, discern, and think deeply about selecting the men and women who march us into the most beautiful battle we could embark upon in life.

More Than A Title

History and Purpose

I looked up the original purpose of the bridal party. In several articles they describe a similar purpose. In my research of a bridesmaid, I learned that young ladies would dress similarly to the bride for protection and to confuse the evil spirits. Fascinating how much that ties into the idea of being a wedding warrior. This was not affiliated with any specific religion. The bridesmaids would accompany the bride to the groom's village and serve as protection from thieves to get the dowry or try to take the bride herself.

Another belief was having women and men dressed similarly to the bride and groom to confuse evil spirits that meant them harm. The evil spirits would not know who the actual bride and groom were, so they did not know who to target. The wedding party would serve as a covering to the bride and groom and overseers of the gifts so that people wouldn't steal from them as the caravan moved about the celebration. In scripture I found this same procession, "In many-colored robes she is led to the king, with her virgin companions following behind her. With joy and gladness they are led along as they enter the palace of the king." (Psalm 45:14-15, ESV) To me there seems to be a greater reason for this cloud of witnesses.

Specifically, the words *covering* and *protection* stick out to me because those are the job of an intercessor—someone who is standing in the gap or praying for a person, place, group, etc. Many intercessors will put up protection in the spirit realm as protection for those who need it. But that prayer cloak is more covering than a bodyguard could ever be. Prayer offers safety that nothing else does because people connect with a living God who cares and knows exactly what they need. All He asks is that you ask Him for what you need, and according to His sovereignty, He will respond.

There is merit to the origin of this tradition because the enemy and his evil spirits would try to steal and be destructive to anything that represents Christ and the church. That's his job description. *(See John 10:10)*. Although we do not fight the enemy with flesh and blood, we are to fight with the things of the Spirit *(Ephesians 6:12-18)*. The physical representation of a covering was established in the wedding process. How much more now should we be aware and take action both physically and spiritually to be a safeguard against the schemes of the enemy?

This is not an easy thing to do. Wedding warriors might face adversity in the midst of covering someone else. Many people think the enemy will lie down and die, but he is busy trying to puff up his fake authority, so the people covering you will need to push through sometimes. They must break chains of pride, poverty, addiction, idolatry, perversion, jealousy, and so much more. When your wedding party is warring on your behalf, please know this is MORE important than the guestlist for the engagement party.

Please do your makeup trial but make sure you've selected warriors you can be vulnerable with. There is nothing worse than fighting a battle without all the intel when it should be available. This is not the time for unspoken prayer requests and vague struggles. This is why this position is not assigned to any and everybody you know.

Discretion, wisdom, and self-control must be tested for those assigned to your wedding party. Make sure you feel spiritually safe, lending your brokenness to be carried by others.

These will be the people to protect some of the most intimate details of your personal struggles as well as your couple clashes. You want to be sure that the people are not only willing to serve but that they are capable. You would not send an untrained fighter into a professional boxing match or an MMA fight. That would be grossly negligent and downright dangerous. We should be aware enough of our relationships to know that we do not place people in situations for them to fail. That is not being a good friend. We should highlight their strengths and strengthen their weaknesses in a safe environment. Let's use wisdom and people management so that we can all succeed.

Imagine a group of bandits coming to steal all of the wedding presents, and the wedding party did nothing to stop them. That's not a typical picture of American culture, but it is one of spiritual significance. There are things more precious than all the items you've placed on your registry. Your peace, unity, and your protection, to name a few. Study and strategize your wedding party according to God's standard of who your circle should be. Allow the Holy Spirit to guide you into selecting your troops.

There is a process for gaining access to the military. You don't just show up, and even when you do, there is training that you must complete before they put you face to face with a real enemy. During this process, many things can determine your eligibility to continue. There are different ranks based on ability and experience. This is not so that you rank your friends but again to remind you that there is a vetting process for most things in life. The jobs you've worked have some process to ensure you are a good fit.

I am encouraging you to do this with your wedding party because the title holds weight. The title should have a review deeper than affiliation. Years of experience in this care are insufficient service hours to pass this assignment. Be intentional, loving, and honest with these conversations, as exclusion should never become an act of offense. On the other hand, we do not just hire our friends to be our doctors because they care about us.

We want to not only be kind, we want to be equipped. Both are necessary for your success.

More Than A Pretty Face

Spiritual Fruit: Characteristics we know

I assume at this point you may have realized I'm a Christian which is great! If you're not, keep reading. I promise this will aid you. Let me be the first to say I believe in surrounding myself with ATTRACTIVE people. Some of the people closest to me have even called me shallow. How dare they? I like what I like. I want to be around all that is beautiful . I almost text talked because I realize that's a bit childish, maybe even immature, and I am okay with it. The aesthetics of your big day are essential! I have seen those weddings where everyone is a different shape and size, and we did not think that dress through.

If you have arrived and this is not an issue for you, be my guest and skip a couple of lines. Please do not put your Amazonian friend right next to the friend you are always trying to feed. That's not a good look, but I digress.

Looks are important, but let's ensure the beauty is not just skin deep. It would be wonderful to include models who are slightly less attractive than you, but it's imperative that you select women who will have the same spirit of inner beauty. The Holy Spirit works in each of His children differently, but He offers the same fruit to us all.

What does inner beauty look like? Is it not being stuck up? Is it helping the less fortunate, sharing the last piece of pie, or hot wing? Of course, we all have our views, but it's more than their ability to be kind when things seem to be going gravy (that just means good...who doesn't love gravy?). It's more than being there that one time at band camp or when you finally broke off that life-sucking relationship. Don't get me wrong; a wedding warrior will have some of these qualities.

However, inner beauty is more valuable than a natural support system. A wedding warrior will possess natural and spiritual attributes. The easiest way I can describe the spiritual aspect is through the Fruit of the Spirit. It is the group of characteristics that come from being connected to the Holy Spirit. These characteristics do not come naturally to the flesh.

There are nine attributes of fruit of the Spirit (characteristics given by the Holy Spirit, see *Galatians 5:22-25*). We will take a focused look at each of them. These characteristics grow and flow out of you the more you surrender to the Holy Spirit, read the Word of God, and seek His face. They show up in times of joy and sorrow. They cannot be removed by human emotion or circumstance. They are steady and life-giving when life seems to have taken all you can give. You can operate in the Fruit of the Spirit because you are connected to Him, empowering you to do what you could never do in the flesh (in your own strength). Let's explore more details about each fruit and how to identify what it looks like in a person, a potential wedding warrior.

Love

Going back a few verses before the Fruit of the Spirit in Galatians 5 talks about loving your neighbor as yourself. How do we love ourselves? One of the ways we do that best is by staying connected with the true source of power. When we stay in a relationship with the creator of the universe, we opt into the most important, life-giving act of self-care. We cannot truly love apart from God, who is love according to 1 John 4:16. God doesn't just love; love is who God is. When we see love in action from the Father, we see Him give His only begotten son. I don't know about you, but I am not too keen on giving my last and only. But this is the type of sacrificial love that God the Father shows us.

The next person in the Trinity (Godhead) shows sacrificial love by giving up His will for the Father's perfect will. We often are generous, kind, and even understanding of a situation or circumstance until it affects our lives. We are fine with growth and sacrifice unless it messes up our schedule. Jesus asks the Father to take the cup of death on the cross from him. This is by far one of the cruelest, most humiliating deaths a person could experience, but the Bible states that death, even death on a cross, could not be compared to the joy set before Him. That joy is the POSSIBILITY that we would receive this gift and be reunited with Jesus for eternity. Another scripture talks about the love of a friend.

John 15:13 reads, *"Greater love has no one than this, that someone lay down his life for his friends."* I am pretty sure we won't need to take any bullets during this wedding process, but I wanted to paint love as the sacrificial act it truly is. We have so many opportunities to watch people suffer without helping or jumping in because it might affect our lives too much, but that is the definition of love. Sacrifice. Love causes you to move into action.

The loving character of God, the Father, caused the Father to give, it caused the Son to die instead of you and me, and love causes the Holy Spirit to empower us to do the same for one another. Unfortunately, when we think about love in this day in age, it has been trampled by this transactional self-service. I encourage you to choose people who exhibit the opposite. You will need people standing by your side to not faint for the joy set before them. *The joy set before you.* You will desire this person to sacrifice their time, talent, and treasure to make sure you have what you need for the relationship as well as the wedding day. We use the word love in the United States freely, but we do not typically give love the respect and gravity it deserves as it is an action word, relentlessly driving God and man to each other's hearts.

What does it look like to love? Real love is driving your friend to the airport at 3 AM on a weekday. Real love is stepping out of comfort to ensure your friend is okay. Real love is driving 13 hours to see your friend on a ration of sleep. Real love is calling to pray with your friend even if you're upset with them because you were led by Holy Spirit to do so. There is a whole chapter in the Bible describing what love is.

"Love is patient and kind; love does not envy or boast; it is not arrogant or rude. It does not insist on its own way; it is not irritable or resentful; it does not rejoice at wrongdoing but rejoices with the truth. Love bears all things, believes all things, hopes all things, endures all things. Love never ends..." (1 Corinthians 13:4-8, ESV)

Love is rejoicing with your friend who got the promotion, engagement, or house even though you were aiming for those things and did not receive them. Love is answering the call to show up when it's convenient but even more so when it's inconvenient. Do you think it was convenient for the Lord to strip Himself down to human form to save us? I'm going to go with it was probably more comfortable for Jesus to be chillin' in the throne room in Heaven with His Father. Our Father. Love causes action. Compassion causes us to spring into the movement toward someone else's need or aid. Look for those who spring into action when you're doing well and especially when you are not.

<u>Fellas</u>: Love can be as simple as your buddy grabbing your food when he goes out or as complicated in correcting behavior unbecoming of a man of God. Love is pushing each other in the gym to do that one extra rep because the goal is to be ripped for the honeymoon. Love might be taking time to be your accountability partner who actually checks up to see if you're still on the narrow path. Men have a way of showing love that might be very different from the ladies, but the fruit is there. The

Word says greater love has none than this, that a man would lay down his life for his friend. Laying down your life can look different in this season, but the one who has sacrificed for you is the one who has shown love.

I have seen men spring into action when there is a harmful situation to their physical bodies, but I would encourage you to select men who will step in when there is the potential for spiritual harm. Showing up can present in so many ways. Beyond the awkwardness of stopping what you are doing to pray about something that is ailing you or bothering you is the type of display I encourage you to look for. As you identify these men, be mindful of their actions being consistent and not that one time they really came through. I hope this also encourages you to be this person not only to your wife but also to your friends. Let the characteristic of love run rampant in your circle.

The men that you call brother because they have your back through thick and thin. The man that you have fallen out with and gone through the steps of reconciliation. This is the type of person that you really need around you both in the wedding and beyond because He understands the importance of relationships and forgiveness. Let's be honest. He was probably right in the first place, but you each caring enough to rectify the situation is the example and the display of love that you really need.

Ladies: Looking for love in all the right places. What can I say? Women have a special ability to love one another in a way that is so comforting. We do not always get it right, but we try so hard to be there for one another. You can see this in so many ways. One of which is just LIFE-GIVING conversation—so much healing (if we are Christ centered in our motives) in our discussion. We are really great at encouraging one another. I have several friends who will correct my speech according to the Word of God. I do not always like it, but I know they are correct.

As women, it is easier to speak life over our friends than over ourselves.

We get this opportunity to be a mirror from Heaven from our friends, reminding each other how God sees us. This is a very common trait among women, but for some, the love shows up a little tougher than others. I will definitely say I have been the tough love friend in my relationships because it is important that you grow. I want to grow, and everything attached to me to grow. This is not the type of love we need all the time, but it is a part of the combination we need.

We see love in practice today in many scenarios. Love can be as simple as making sure you grab your friend's favorite snack when you get your own. It could be checking on her after you know she had a tough day. It might be coming over and letting her cry on you for an hour. It shows up in so many different ways. One of the ways my friend forces her love on me is by making tea for me and waiting until I open up to her about everything. Without fail, she will patiently wait until I break because she knows I can be strong, but I also want to be heard and encouraged even when it is inconvenient.

Showing love to one another as we get older can become a little tricky as our lives get busier, but relationships that stand the test of time will continue to grow. Conversations and quality time may be less, but the connection points are still life-giving when they do happen. I love my group of friends because they never stop pursuing Jesus and will share that pursuit with me as well as them pursuing that love relationship with me. Sacrificing their preferences, time, and energy to make sure that I am well in mind, body, and spirit.

Many times this is the person inquiring about how you are really doing, not settling for the crumbs of the true update that you give in five minutes over coffee. This is also love. Love covers, it inquires it cares and most of all it moves.

Joy

Joy is especially integral because the Bible says, *"The Joy of the Lord is your strength."* (Nehemiah 8:10) In times of difficulty and stress, having someone full of joy, not happiness, is valuable. Happiness is temporal and can be affected by circumstance. Joy can carry you through tough situations because it is found within, not a response to, an external experience. Joy is such an interesting fruit because it propels you to the greater thing that despair and fear are trying to keep you from. There are so many things that can affect our mood and the way we see the world but having true joy is an unshakable anchor to the truth of God's goodness. He is good in any situation and that is a sobering reality that we can always cling to. Clinging to joy is a choice that shifts perspective not to what is going on but the one who is holding it all.

Joy can be a full body experience. It can show up in laughter, dance, in tears or even silence. Joy is fuel for your future that cannot be denied by the things you see around your current reality. Joy is trusting in the evidence of who God is. It is resting in His security. Joy gives you the courage to keep moving forward.

A genuine smile, word of encouragement, or time of laughter can lighten the mood and allow forward motion to become ten times easier. The Bible talks about laughter actually being medicine to our bones. We have a glorious strength that is ever-present. Joy knows that we will not perish. Joy is the response to Salvation. Joy comes from knowing who you are and whose you are. We, believers, get to call the Creator of the universe Abba Father, friend, and comforter. Those realities will never change, and neither will our joy. Joy is based on the eternal realities of love. Speaking of joy, not happiness, we can experience this fallen world and still have the joy of the Lord. When I was about sixteen years old, my family lost our home of nine years. I happened to have a friend over that day from church, and as we were about to go bike riding, the police drove up into our circle driveway. I was an unsuspecting teenager who hadn't experienced anything like this in real life.

Needless to say, we never got to go on that bike ride but instead started packing up the home I'd known for most of my adolescence. My friend and I packed teddy bears, posters, bedding, and clothes. I remember the two of us standing in my baby blue room at the wall closet, bagging the clothes hanging in my closet, when I started to lose it. It felt like my mind was teetering on the brink of insanity. I'd never felt anything like it.

I couldn't rationalize how something I'd only seen in movies was happening to me. Something that I did not contribute to. Something that was not fair. In a moment of fear, confusion, and disbelief, my friend looked at me and said, "Everything is going to be okay."

I know that wasn't a ground-stabilizing statement to most, but it was just what I needed to hear. Her presence in the storm, with her quiet strength and encouragement, allowed me to continue. A bit of a somber moment to exhibit joy, but I would rather show the power of the strength of the Lord when it's needed most. What good does it do to have a life preserver when you're standing in shallow water up to your knees? The power of God is demonstrated most in adversity. The Bible says, *"'...My grace is sufficient for you, for my power is made perfect in weakness.' Therefore I will boast all the more gladly of my weaknesses so that the power of Christ may rest upon me."* (2 Corinthians 12:9)

My friend was led by the Holy Spirit when she stated this simple phrase, and it gave me the strength to keep going. It gave me strength to know that the world would NOT end that day. It's not your typical depiction of joy, I'm sure, but life doesn't always offer smiles and rainbows. However, pure joy offers you the ability to weather any storm because of the strength it provides. Had that friend not been at my side, I am unsure how I would have responded to my crisis. What she said was not by man's standard profound in any way, but it encouraged me to the point of contentment and, ultimately, joy. I was able to keep the majority of my possessions, and most importantly, I hadn't lost my family.

Someone full of joy is not the same as someone happy because happiness is fleeting and can change based on the circumstances. Joy is unshakable and is not supplied by experience. The Holy Spirit strengthens us with joy to continue when things are tough. Joyful people know that there are issues, but their outlook, perspective, and actions differ from those who depend on happiness. A person who harnesses the ability to turn a hopeless situation into one that gives you hope is someone who understands the fullness of joy. This is the kind of warrior I want by my side when entering this beautiful battle.

Fellas: I know joy is not one of those emotions we typically celebrate or associate with men, but it presents in the guy that lights up the room, especially when things are down. He's the guy that drags you out of your comfort zone because you've been working nonstop. He's the one to remind you that there is joy in the little things and the quiet moments. Joy is exemplified in the guy who makes the entire room fill with laughter when things are tense. This man keeps moments that could become hostile, hilarious. When things are tough, this is the man you want to be around because he will identify the silver lining in any situation. This is not someone unaware of the realities of life, just a man who refuses to let circumstances change the reality of his position as a son, king, priest, and fellow heir to Christ Jesus.

Ladies: So many times, we look at joy and characterize it as happiness, but the two could not be farther from each other. We all know that girl who is always bubbly with a giant smile on her face. My question to you is, what is that lovely countenance motivated by? Is it motivated by the current absence of stress, or is it her focus on the Lord that allows her to focus on Him throughout the storm? Does she react well when things are going her way, or is she polite, full of hope that all her needs will be met according to the Word of God regardless of the circumstances?

Joy is such a beautiful display of our trust in the Father. I know that joy can show up when things are beautiful, but much like peace, we need joy when things are far from great. When we see that friend whose life is falling apart, but she is going about her life secure in the fact that the Lord has her so that she can smile. This is not a facade but a genuine strength from the Lord that allows you to laugh in the midst of trial and smile through adversity. It's like this knowing that no matter what life or the enemy throws at you, you know that God is in control and that He is working it out for your good so you can rest. You can rest because you know that the Creator has you in His hands and that your destiny is secure. There is joy in knowing your Heavenly Father has the final say about your life, and you can show that to others. Your friend or sister in Christ who exhibits this quality is the person you need in your wedding party. She will remind you that you need to have fun, especially when things seem to be going awry. She will encourage you that the Lord has the final say. We can be confident in this as believers, and she will specifically be the person to bring that to the forefront when things are the toughest.

Peace

We all know that person who brings a sense of calm and security to every situation. This might be the friend that you usually call and ask for help or when your world seems to be falling apart. She is typically the one you invite to get things pleasant and under control. If you don't, I suggest you pray for a friend who embodies this. is extremely valuable because there will be times in the wedding planning process and beyond when the clarity of calm will be beneficial. Peace is integral to the wedding and maintaining a friendship after the BIG DAY. I have heard and seen at least a few times where something simple put a wedge in between the friendship bonds that were so evident before the wedding. This offense and tearing away is NOT necessary. As children of God, we need to have strong people of faith in our lives. It is a shame to see those relationships broken over something that more calm and understanding would explain in love.

We all want to keep the 'Bridezilla' tucked away in her castle. Peace is one of the fruits needed to keep that on lockdown. Peace will put out a lot of the fires our mouths tend to start because of pressure. If you have no clue what I am talking about, think about the 'hot head' in the group and some of the things they would say that could be offensive. I am not saying don't make her a bridesmaid but make sure she brings something to the table that does not add stress. Sometimes watching these women at work is fun when a situation needs more vibrato.

However, there needs to be an environment that cultivates a tension-free atmosphere. A bridesmaid bearing this characteristic of the fruit of the Spirit does not mean you all will not have issues, but there will be a sense of wholeness and safety that only a person calm under fire can provide. Just picture Jesus on the boat with the disciples when there was a terrible storm, and Jesus was taking a nap (No, I'm not saying he was aloof. I am saying He was not bothered by the circumstance).

When the disciples woke Him, He simply said, *'Peace be still,'* and it says that there was a great calm (Mark 4:35-39). I don't imagine your wedding warrior will walk around saying peace be still, but I do expect her to use the authority given by almighty God to take a situation that is out of control and bring it to calm. This woman's very presence will shift the atmosphere or feeling of a room without effort.

I can be pretty intense when stressed, and I usually need someone who sees beyond the present moment and the present trial to offer me a plate of peace for my worry. Sometimes stress is not a result of an outside force but an inside force. It's not always that ladies were late getting their dresses. The menu or the venue had a snag. It can be our own anxiety that sends us into a tailspin or the need to control every aspect sending us into unrest.

We, as believers, forget the fact that worry is a sin. It is evidence that our trust is in ourselves, the people around us, or the things the world can provide, not in GOD. This is so dangerous because people generally think they can control life. I am here to tell you that if that were true, I would be in a very different state. I had plans to be so much more than I currently am now. I had plans to have completed a four year degree at age twenty-two and be managing some amazing bands by now. I had plans to be better and financially self-sufficient, and those are both goals that I strive for, but I cannot allow myself to lose my top every time a plan goes unrealized.

I am in a season where God is challenging my trust. It is easier said than done to truly trust and depend on Him. It is a dependence on the character of God that I have never had to walk in before. One of the things that I can say is that His peace has greatly been a theme in this season as I learn how to trust Him deeper. It is a peace that makes no sense. It is a peace that is all-encompassing and ready to cast down every bit of man's logic and knowledge for the reality of the Kingdom of Heaven.

We can enter peace when we let go and rest in our Father's arms. The wedding warrior who is strong in this gift will understand and be able to explain and recreate this space. They walk within the strength of peace, calling everything to bow to the authority of Heaven. The people well versed in this characteristic of the fruit of the Spirit tend to magnify the Lord. It is the discipline to see and *behold God* larger than anything else competing for our attention. When we lose focus on our Heavenly Father, we magnify things that have no place in our purview.

The strange thing about putting your trust in others is that they will always let you down. I wouldn't even say intentionally, but because people are not perfect, they will always fail our expectations. People were not meant to take the throne of God, and when we hold them to that standard, they come up short. When we put our trust in man, they cannot live up to God-sized responsibilities even if they want to. The Lord desires people to rest in Him and utilize His peace. In John 14:27, Jesus says that He will leave His peace with us so that we will not worry or be fearful. Jesus, the man who willingly went to the cross to pay a debt He did not owe, gives us His peace of mind. This fact is something to be treasured because He walked the road to His death carrying a heavy burden but did not stress or worry. There are a few more scripture references that are usually partially quoted. One is He will keep you in perfect peace (Isaiah 26:3), and the other is peace that passes all understanding (Philippians 4:7).

These scripture verses have more to offer than the cliches they've become. Take Isaiah, for example. Verse three says, "You keep him in perfect peace whose mind is stayed on you because he trusts in you." Verse four says, "Trust in the LORD forever, for the LORD GOD is an everlasting rock."

So there is a way to maintain perfect peace. Keeping your mind focused on the Lord and placing your trust in Him. The bridesmaid or groomsman who is well-learned in this quality will usher in God's stillness and quiet strength and remind the bride-to-be to continually place her trust in Christ, the solid rock. The other verse in Philippians explains that God will give you peace that passes all understanding surely enough. It also teaches us two huge benefits resulting from that peace: Verse six, "Do not be anxious about anything, but in everything by prayer and supplication with thanksgiving let your requests be made known to God." Verse seven, "And the peace of God, which surpasses all understanding, WILL guard your hearts and your minds in Christ Jesus."

Again the Lord is encouraging us not to worry or have anxiety about anything. Literally nothing. Instead, he instructs us to be thankful and ask Him for our desires. In His process, we must thankfully ask (communicate in prayer) and not worry. After we have done this, we place our trust in the Lord to respond on our behalf. He will assure us that whatever His response, His peace will actually cause our hearts and minds to be safe because we've placed it in His hands. If you think about it, God's peace is instrumental in our physical body and mental state. Therefore, a wedding warrior bearing this quality will benefit not only the environment in which you plan your wedding day but also your physical and mental state.

We talk about the scripture instructing us to guard our hearts above all else because from it flows the issues of life, but no one really says how to guard it. In this instance, understanding that we aren't actually able to guard our hearts, but it is a true surrender to the will of God that protects our hearts from being punctured to the point of no return. I understand more and more that peace is not the absence of chaos but standing in the Lord's protection that allows us to go unscathed by our circumstances. I understand things hurt us, and in difficult situations, life can seem to be crippling.

Life has a way of pressing so hard that we second guess God's will and question our ability and purpose, but peace brings clarity to move forward or keep standing still until the next steps are revealed. The person who excels in carrying the gift of peace will be able to bring soundness to the roar of life not only in this season of your life but those to come. For example, when the kids are screaming, your workload is a week behind, and you have not had a real conversation with your husband in two weeks. We tend to reach out to those who are close to those who seem the most accessible, but those people are not always the ones who can help bring God's peace to your storm.

Fellas: You know the guy who is always encouraging you to chill when things are getting heated on the court? Or the guy who is telling the group to knock it off when the jokes are hitting a little too close to home?

This guy comes across as meek, but most men tend to think of this characteristic as a weakness. Meekness is strength under control. He will have the elegant ability to cut through the foolishness of rage or corrupt speech and maintain a sense of order and calm. This guy is typically the peacemaker and the one who is inclusive. He may be a little more in tune with the emotional temperature of the group. You will want to look for these characteristics, especially if you have a more rowdy group. He will be able to move the wing sauce from hot to mild.

Ladies: The lady you choose with this characteristic will show certain attributes. If you've been in a situation where you are so mad that you cannot think, this friend comes to you and almost instantly calms you down. Her presence alone makes you remember that your emotions are getting the best of you, and you need to bring your focus back to Christ. Peace is not the absence of adversity but the environment where those who operate in the fruit of peace tend to stand out. She will be able to speak peace to the circumstances and the group going through the wedding process and peace to your mind as you walk through nor tumultuous days of your marriage. She will not encourage your temper tantrums or your extended periods of worry. She will help you remember that there is so much to be grateful for and remind you that Jesus is the prince of peace. She will remind you that Jesus leaves His peace with us.

The Characteristics We Don't Pray For

Patience

Patience is a beautiful word that people say is a virtue. It is a virtue, so let's look deeper at what patience is. While digging into the Word, I found that patience was interchangeable with endurance. Another definition *(HELPS Word-studies)* speaks about the ability to remain. The ability to remain through trials and stress should be something we hope to have in the wedding mix. Patience is instrumental because the person who possesses this quality can endure hard times. The Bible speaks about God's endurance in Romans 15:5. May the God of endurance and encouragement grant you to live in such harmony with one another in accord with Christ Jesus.

The one who possesses this attribute will be able to endure and encourage you. In some versions of the Bible, patience is referred to as long-suffering. Hopefully, as the bride, you will do your best to minimize suffering. However, the ability to withstand hardship is what patience is. A patient person exemplifies their faith and believes the end will be better than its beginning. They are aware that the outcome is worth the discomfort.

Much like Christ as He suffered in agony just to redeem us. He was more than capable of saving Himself from the physical pain and being forsaken by His Father so that we could be reunited with our Heavenly Father. The outcome of His suffering on Calvary did not compare with the joy to come *(see Ecclesiastes 7:8).*

Patience is not one of my strengths. I guess I should say that I am being challenged and grown into the fruit of patience. I have been the Christian who vowed never to pray for this patience because I do not want to be tested. Whether that is right or wrong, I don't know, and I do not dare ask. I know that patience is a Fruit of the Spirit I desperately need around me, and I imagine it is extremely important in the wedding process. Stress tends to make me snippy, and I will need someone with the patience of Job to be by my side.

Let's be crystal clear about this subject. I had to be patient with myself while writing this. I have a confession to make: I am not actually a writer. I am just being obedient to sharing content the Lord sees fit to share. I had to sit down for years to complete this work of art or this hopeful work of art. Patience is a wonder; it takes faith and hope to believe that the present is worth the outcome. The thing about trust is that there are levels. I have learned that the trust that got me through tough times in the past is not fit to carry me through the next trial. As we grow in our faith and move through our lives we must trust the Lord more and more. He will reveal the areas where we are lacking trust and challenge us to lean into his arms more through patience. Patience causes us to wait on the Lord and trust that He still desires good things for us because we are His kids. The wedding warrior who understands this will be able to encourage you in the midst of uncertainty because they firmly trust in the Lord.

The crazy thing about me is that I can sense when I am getting impatient, and I can choose at that moment to give over to the roughness or harness that my flesh craves or lend myself to the Spirit. The outcome rarely changes based on our impatient actions. There tend to be more feelings hurt, fender benders, and messes to fix but not truly a different outcome. So being around someone who is able to bring me back to reality is a huge asset. When I am out of character it does nothing to fix my actual problem in these moments. We can dwell on all the things we so desperately wanted to arrive but the anxiety does not do a thing to help. It may raise our blood pressure or encourage us to eat more of the non-diet foods we knew we had no business eating. Knowing that impatience is birthed out of fear should prompt us to see the enemy's schemes trying to get us to act before its time.

Right now, this is a huge lesson for me. I have been without a vehicle for about three months, and it is entirely FRUSTRATING, but my patience in this season will lend greater results than operating out of a place of worry. I desire something specific. Much like I hope you desired something specific in your spouse. You could have chosen to marry the first man who said you were attractive, but I'm going to go out on a limb and say that is not most of our stories. Waiting is a part of God's story. It seems so unnecessary, but that is the place where God himself tends to have our attention the most. The gift of patience is God's anchor to His perfect will for our lives.

Earlier this week, I asked a friend to pray for me. One of the things he felt God wanted to share with me was, "remain patient with me as I have been patient with you". That hit me like a ton of bricks. The Lord remains extremely patient with me, but that's not what I typically focus on. How beautiful a display. The perfect one said give me some time to work on your behalf. This reminds me how quickly I can run headfirst into my problems without consulting Him. There is even patience to slow down enough to include God in all we do. Hopefully, I will grow in this characteristic of the fruit of the Spirit and have the grace to wait (Proverbs 25:15). With patience, a ruler may be persuaded, and a soft tongue will break a bone.

Fellas: We've all heard the jokes about the patience of Job, but we don't often use him as a model of patience. Patience, also known as long-suffering, is a very special fruit. Mainly because not many people desire to suffer. It's not one of those things our society thinks of as sexy or appealing. So to use Job as an example, he was extremely wealthy, but at the allowance of the Lord, most everything was stripped away from him, including his children, wealth, and his health. All of this, and yet he did NOT curse God. He cursed the day he was born, but he dared not question the goodness of God even though he was encouraged by his wife and had the negativity of his friends toward him.

So what does this look like in today's society? I'd say the man who shows characteristics of patience would be the one who tends to reach out to the guy who takes a little more energy to be around. Or the person who knows that none of you will show up on time but waits patiently fifteen minutes before time because that's his nature. He does not complain even though he would be well within his right to do so. There are so many people that take this person for granted, but they are consistently showing up when you need them. They will be present and encouraging even when you are not those things for yourself. The man who excels in patience will not just give you advice but also the space to process and hear directly from the Lord.

Ladies: Whew, well, this might be a little stereotypical, but the woman who displays patience may be the one who cooks you a spread. I say this because cooking involves so much preparation and patience that most do not delight in the process. The way I view patience is as something that might take hours to simmer to the perfect result. This is not someone who runs to the quickest solution. The lady who operates in this gift will pause and take a second before responding to the crazy story you just told. This person will take a breath before possibly responding in hot anger. The woman who is accustomed to long suffering will be the one who gently nudges you that you need to leave thirty minutes, fifteen minutes, five minutes, and stops nudging after a while because it will do more to irritate the group than help move them forward. She will remain present with you when you are in your weakest and wait out the storm with you.

Kindness

"You is kind. You is smart. You is important."
Look here. I promise you this is not always my strong suit. I am a straight shooter, and the more pressure I'm under, the less honey coated my words become. For the record I am working on it, I have a scripture posted on my bathroom mirror reminding me to speak gracious words that are sweet and healing to the bones. When I reflect on my personality and my relationship with Christ I tell people, please be glad I know Jesus. I really aspire to be kind, but this is not a word I would typically use to describe myself. It's not because I'm not nice or kind, but some people are SUPER KIND like it's their superpower! You know the people I'm talking about. The ones who let every rude comment, assault on their personality, or their time roll off their backs with a sunny disposition. Almost like their smile is their armor. It's crazy to watch a person walk in such kindness. It's **God-powered**, which causes me to stand in awe. Needless to say, this characteristic of the fruit of the Spirit is a necessity!

If you are the person who carries this, I applaud you. We need you to duplicate yourself a million times over. Seriously if you could work on that, it'd be great! These people are so considerate and always look for ways to make things easier. Kindness is something we rarely experience in our daily lives but is so appreciated when it is directed our way. We tend to call it out in complete strangers when they show compassion. The way kindness can warm your heart through a simple act is unreal.

How often do we call it out, see it, and use it in our inner circle? This one might be sitting right under your nose. Begin to call that kindness out when you experience it, and you will see who walks this path. The

Holy Spirit really works through these people as He empowers us to love our enemies. Scripture tells us, *"If your enemy is hungry, give him bread to eat, and if he is thirsty, give him water to drink, for you will heap burning coals on his head, and the Lord will reward you". (Proverbs 25:21-22, ESV)*

This is the love God shows in a very practical, KIND way. I don't know the last time you baked your enemies a fresh batch of cookies, but it would be kind to do so. The Bible speaks about showing this kindness in requesting something over and over. Showing kindness is not something that a person exhibiting kindness always feels like doing, but it is something they operate in to show the love of Christ. We don't want to only be kind in large gestures. We also want to be kind in the minute 'insignificant' gestures. Treating your waitstaff with dignity, respect, honor, and generosity is a way to ensure kindness is shown. What if everyone involved in your wedding process had a great 'people' experience? What if every life your wedding party touched left with the impression, wow, those are some of the kindest people I've ever encountered.

What if planning your wedding positively impacted your world to bring them into the saving knowledge of Christ? We want to be people who truly DISPLAY the loving kindness of Christ. This person can help you not only be kind to those closest to you when emotions run high, but they can help you witness every person you encounter.

Fellas: You know the guy who is always looking out for you and the other guys? The guy who will not only give the homeless person resources but also his time in conversation. Pay attention to the one picking up the tab or always offer to help out even when it is inconvenient. Someone kind is NOT a pushover, but they are someone who draws you in with the kindness of Christ. He makes you feel apart when you're new. He checks on you when you haven't been to hang in a while. This guy is genuinely interested in your well-being which may be a little creepy considering not many people are like this, but if it's genuine, welcome it, and don't cast it off.

Ladies: You know that woman who is always thinking of others in their daily life? The one who will randomly call or text you with encouragement? This is the type of woman who you will want to surround yourself with. A woman who is kind will be able to intentionally sense how to be selfless at the moment and draw you back to Jesus. The kindness of God is responsible for leading us to repentance. It's not the friend telling you everything wrong but encouraging you to keep doing the things you are doing well.

Goodness

This characteristic is one that the Lord uses to describe Himself a lot in scripture. I can quote so many scriptures on goodness but is goodness an inherent thing we know to be true? How would you define good? There is a scripture where Jesus questions a man who calls him good. Jesus says, *"And Jesus said to him, "Why do you call me good? No one is good except God alone." (Luke 18:19, ESV)* Webster's Dictionary defines "good" as "better, best, morally excellent...righteous."

The Word also says, *"none is righteous, no, not one" (Romans 3:10)*, so how are we even to attain this virtue? I am getting the revelation on this characteristic as I type. We tend to forget about this characteristic of the fruit of the Spirit. I am seeing the weightiness of allowing the Lord to work this through you.

As scripture states, we are not good. I know that assaults my pride, as I am sure it does yours. We tend to say phrases like he's a good person even though (fill in the blank) or I don't follow God, and I'm still a good person. I get the rationale, but we can only do good things if we are connected to the Father. Every person can tap into their God connection as we are made in the image of God. Goodness is in the DNA of our souls to crave and give, but the essence of GOOD can only come from God.

We recognize goodness, but we cannot produce it on our own. This brings to mind the verse Matthew 7:11, *"If you then, who are evil, know how to give good gifts to your children, how much more will your Father who is in Heaven give good things to those who ask him!"* This proves that we desire good for others and ourselves, even if we are evil. So back to the question: how do we achieve this without being connected to the source?

I would say we can't. So the person who exhibits this attribute of the Spirit will be in tune with the Father and connected to the heart of God. We cannot consistently operate in a place of goodness without experiencing the goodness of God or being connected to His heart. Goodness is one of the things the Lord asks us to try Him in. It's like He's saying sweetie, you cannot be around me and leave the same. My goodness will touch you and change you for the better. It reminds me of the scripture. *"Oh, taste and see that the Lord is good!"*. (Psalm 34:8)

Excuse my hood moment. The Lord challenges us to pull up on Him and see if He will leave us better, best, morally excellent, righteous. I can honestly say I have never encountered His presence without this happening. Who in your life exemplifies this character? When you leave them, do you feel fuller, stronger, better, more hopeful, lighter, refreshed? I would say that this is the person who walks out goodness.

Fellas: So the guy who finds a $50 bill in the locker room and searches to find the rightful owner. You know he has a date a little later and could have used that money to impress her a bit more. It may be uncomfortable to be his friend sometimes because he will go out of his way to ensure the right thing is done. He is a Boy Scout/Eagle Scout in his personality. He serves others above his ambitions, allowing the golden rule to guide his life and actions. He allows the Holy Spirit to guide his reactions, not his flesh. This man will be helpful to make sure the character of Christ is upheld in your business dealings and your personal life.

Ladies: She might be the woman you call the rule follower. She may go out of her way to make sure everyone feels special even though she doesn't know everyone. She will be the one to remind you that it is still good on Earth and that humanity touched by the Lord can be beautiful. This lady will speak well of those around her and walk in a way that is influenced by the Word of God. Because goodness is a God characteristic, this person will be well versed in the Word and allow Christ to guide her actions. She will encourage you to live this way with her and bring a specific standard to how your wedding party interacts with one another and those serving.

The Characteristics We Neglect

Gentleness

As I write this portion of the book, I am reminded that I need to approach it gently. There is such strength in the gentleness that is beautiful and sweet to the soul. I do not often hear this about myself. It is a characteristic that requires great balance and control. I say this because it is not a position of weakness. It is one of power. When one is gentle, it is a choice to show the love of Christ through restraint. Gentleness carries the wisdom to sway without crashing waves.

The person who operates in gentleness has the ability to steer the ship without turning it over. As I write, I am so grateful for the revelation of this attribute because I have looked at this as a point of weakness in the past when it is the exact opposite. I hope to have a gentle heart and tongue, but it is not always my go-to. We must value this characteristic because of the small corrections to create big change. Say it again for the people in the back.

"*For we all stumble in many ways. And if anyone does not stumble in what he says, he is a perfect man, able also to bridle his whole body. If we put bits into the mouths of horses so that they obey us, we also guide their whole bodies. Look at the ships also: though they are so large and driven by strong winds, they are guided by a tiny rudder wherever the pilot's will directs. So also the tongue is a small member, yet it boasts of great things. How great a forest is set ablaze by such a small fire." (James 3:2-5, ESV)*

If we truly are guided by the Spirit, we will use our mouths to speak the Word of God and to encourage. Gentleness is one of the things that show up in many aspects of our lives. The way we drive on an icy road or the way we handle a baby. Gentleness is a great responsibility in order to protect the very thing that has been entrusted to you. As we walk in gentleness, we must discern timing.

One of my favorite scriptures is Galatians 6:1 which encourages us who are spiritual to restore others in a spirit of gentleness. What does that look like? It is less bashing one over the head for poor decisions and more of encouraging a person to find the motive for the wrong action through introspection. The sky is green can immediately be dismissed because of the straightforward nature of the statement.

However, if I were to ask you what color the sky is and your response was green, I could ask you to explain why the sky is green to understand your reasoning. You are more inclined to be open and receptive to explaining yourself than if you were told to get your life together. We must also be able to take straightforward corrections, it is also necessary to be course-corrected in other ways, as this is how the Lord corrects us. *The LORD has appeared of old to me, saying: "Yes, I have loved you with everlasting love. Therefore, with lovingkindness, I have drawn you. (Jeremiah 31:3)*

<u>**Fellas**</u>: I realize that this one might be a bit of a struggle because American culture has characterized gentleness as a feminine trait. I also understand that there are areas where it's natural for men to be gentle. So key into a few examples of what to look for in a groomsman who carries this trait. One is how a man treats his daughter, sister, or mother. He does not approach them like he approaches the guys in his life. This can be seen in little boys to grandfathers and their granddaughters.

One of the other situations you can see this care and compassion in men is with food. I know big reveal, but the image from carefully carrying in pizza and groceries to moving the turkey on Thanksgiving day from the oven to the dining table. You cherish your food, so you're careful to ensure it reaches its proper destination. These seem funny, but without real direction, it is a space where extra care and consideration come naturally.

Another way I want to point out gentleness is with a brand-new vehicle. Most men will treat their new cars like newborn babies. They might park away from all the other vehicles in the lot. They will wash and wax the car at a hint of dirt.

So now we know that men can show gentleness. How does that show up in our day-to-day lives in a spiritual context? The man who is sensitive to the Word of God. This guy will reverence the Word or the presence of God not from a place of religion but relationship. When it's time to speak about some of the more serious topics of life, he might be more careful not to joke around. He will not smack you (or whoever it is) with the Word in correction. He will be sensitive to the timing and your mental and emotional state when delivering the rebuke. This is so needed in the body as a part of accountability. It's hard enough to be corrected, but we tend to run into issues when it is done with no real caution or concern for your personhood.

Ladies: Gentleness comes "naturally" to us. We are generally considered nurturers but, I would dare to say that we need to be in the space of vulnerability to share gentleness with others, especially other adults. It is easy to be gentle with people and things we determine should be handled with care. I will be honest with my personality. You will typically get-tough love first. So people have been cautious about coming to me with things they think are silly or do not deserve that level of care. This is not my intention, but there are ways I can show those around me a more gentle side. The person who operates in the spirit of gentleness carries it with them. The way she approaches situations, people, and even altercations will be that of a gentle spirit. This will be so important to your wedding party and your marriage as this will cause you to communicate and live in a way that draws your husband to you and Christ.

It takes a lot of strength to be gentle. You must select a woman who stays in the Word and has an active prayer life because it is almost impossible to be gentle in positions that call for a human response of frustration or anger. You have to stay connected to the source and walk with him to see his perspective of the situation to operate the way He would.

Self-Control

Self-control is one of the most difficult things for people to accomplish, mainly because it's contrary to our flesh. We are spiritual beings first wrapped in flesh, but we often struggle to deny the flesh because it's easier to understand. Back to self-control.

One of the best examples I can give is with food. You know when you're at your favorite dessert shop, and it's your birthday, but you just vowed to lose thirty pounds. It's not that you cannot or should not indulge, but how much you should indulge is the real question. I hope I'm growing in this area, but this is more or less a test when you're either really comfortable or under pressure.

As I sit here writing this, I am TEMPTED to walk right back into Mother Road Market and get a chicken sandwich or a slice of pizza. I haven't eaten (natural food) in a day and a half. The Lord called me to fast for a few days. Not something I really enjoy. It is a spiritual discipline that keeps me close to the Lord. Also, there is a difference between being tempted and acting on that temptation. Sometimes we like to bundle them like the internet. Okay, I tried to be funny (What if it were socially acceptable to add emojis to books?). I digress.

Having and operating well in self-control is not ever having temptation but being able to say no when you *don't* want to. It's as simple as knowing you should not have that second donut or as deep as knowing I like this person, but I know things could get out of hand if we're in this type of environment. Knowing that Holy Spirit, our guide and comforter, can see where our actions will lead and leaning into His gentle nudging is where self-control thrives. I'll be honest sometimes I don't 'know' when to stop, or I'm simply not paying attention.

You can talk too much, do too much, consume too much. The stopping point for things is where we have to be sensitive and obedient to Holy Spirit's prompting. When we don't we run the risk of injury either to ourselves or others. This is why you need to have this characteristic of the fruit of the Spirit active in one of the people in your wedding party. You will want to lean into this person for budgeting, making sure you can fit into your dress, and your language etc. Our words create realities and cannot be unspoken.

The person who has self-control in the bag is able to truly assist you in not going over the top (unless that's your aesthetic, but still, there's a limit). I hope to benefit from this attribute because I have a very generous heart, and I am not always sure when to stop. It doesn't just have to be financial. We can bend over backward for people, even on our big day, to the point that it stresses us out, and we neglect the joy of the moment.

The person who exhibits this characteristic will be able to curb the extremes of desires both on the wedding day and in the days to come. Imagine going out for the first time with your friends after you've come up for air from the honeymoon. You're telling all the stories, but you know your spouse is a little more private than you. The person with self-control might want to know all the details but can give you a look or steer the conversation into a safer place. They are able to be your bowling bumpers to keep you in the lane and help you get all the strikes (good in bowling, bad in baseball).

We've all seen an episode of *Bridezilla*. Most of the time, the most shocking act was how the bride spoke with her bridesmaids or others. If you tend to fly off the handle verbally, you NEED this person not only in your wedding, you need them in your life. I have worked hard at growing in this area. My family can still get me off the rails pretty quickly, but I have friends who will objectively sit and listen, mediate, and correct both sides. For the sake of all your relationships after the wedding day, I advise you to put some stock in this area.

There was a time when my father and I would argue to the death. Well obviously not to the death but you get the point. I remember one argument in particular where we started talking, then shouting then screaming. I realized that the slightest raise in my father's volume caused me to escalate but I wanted to be heard. Shortly after the argument was over I realized my voice was actually affected. During this time the Lord was speaking to me about my giftings and showing me more clearly how He would operate through me. The majority of the things I am called to do involve my voice. I sing, encourage and share messages with people from God's prompting. After this argument I could not sing above a tenor voicing. At the time I had soprano parts in an acapella group. My voice was gone for several weeks because I did not operate in self control. Instead of praying or de-escalating the situation I added fuel to the fire and it burned me. I promise the return on a self-control investment will be worth it.

Fellas: So this one right here. this characteristic of the fruit of the Spirit is almost rare in today's day and age, but it is there. You may have to look a little harder to locate the man operating in this characteristic. If you already know who he is, I encourage you to get close to him. This is COUNTERCULTURAL. We have to catch these gems as soon as we identify them. Some practical ways to find this guy might be in the way/amount your friends are eating. I am not asking for the steroid popping; I pick things up and put things down, gym junkie. I am talking about the I eat clean, but I am aware I shouldn't have that extra piece of cake and then not eat it. I am talking about the guy who sets clear boundaries and sticks to them in relationships with his friend and girlfriend/spouse. The man who gets a reasonable amount of sleep most of the time. These things seem practical, but I want to show how to spot these potential people.

Ladies: Self-control is one of those things that we aren't typically thrilled about if we are being honest. It is a level of self-denial that we would rather go without. However, there is usually that one girl in your group of friends who is excellent at it. One of the ways it is easy for us ladies to show self-control is in what we say and what we do not. Considering that women speak twice as many words as men on average, this might be a challenge. We all had that moment of self-correction once we started a juicy story and then had to choose to continue or not based on our self-control. Yes, it would be the talk of the group chat for the next two weeks but is that worth hurting your friend or destroying the trust of those who spoke to you in confidence? The young lady who operates in this gift might not even bring this type of topic up as it is genuinely gossip and not information everyone needs to know.

Your friend with self-control is the girl you invite to the mall or any other shopping escapade to keep you on your budget. She is the friend who warns against impulse buying and offers to help you budget. Sis, let me say if you are on a budget and need to stay on track, you NEED this woman. I understand this is not the most fun limitation to put on yourself, but I promise your bank account and your husband will be grateful for the sacrifice. You need self-control in all aspects of your life, whether it be food, finances, communication, etc. Please do not discount this person because they can speak into areas of your life for years to come. Through Holy Spirit, she will give you practical tools for biblical living.

A woman with a strength of self-control will be able to ensure that there is balance and privacy concerning issues that should remain close to the vest. A woman led by Holy Spirit in this area will not encourage you to eat or drink your feelings. She will depend on the Word of God to be the measuring stick to which we are to live our lives. She will remind you of your commitment to purity with your fiancé and media. She will be able to encourage your bachelorette party not to be too risque.

This is not typically the person you enjoy inviting to the party because they desire moderation. The Lord wants us to celebrate but not at the expense of becoming morally corrupt. At the stage of marriage, you would desire this trait as you want to be an example with your relationship as well as your individual life. This person helps to keep that on track.

Faithfulness

Faithfulness in Hebrew can be translated as Emunah- trusting, firmness, steadfastness, and truth. This characteristic is especially important to me because it is part of what my name means. (Faithful Friend). Faithfulness is not easy to carry out because of the quiet strength it requires. I remember asking the Lord about friendship and my name some years ago. I did not often receive the same care from the people I considered friends. They were not terrible people, but I'm wired a little bit differently. I wondered if I would ever have a person take the same amount of consideration for our relationship as I did. During that conversation, the Lord started dealing with me on faithfulness. He simply stated that to be faithful I had to be FULL of FAITH. I know it doesn't exactly sound profound, but it stood out to me because I only thought of being faithful in a physical sense. I thought of faithfulness as having a large stone that would never be shaken, like a constant stream, steady and quiet.

These are great examples of what faithfulness is, but the question I did not ask was, how could I translate that to a person? Stones and streams do not have emotions or a way to communicate, but I did and still do. The key to my ability to be faithful in anything is having faith or belief that the situation or relationship would get better or grow without seeing the evidence.

Jonathan and David in the Bible are a great example of a faithful friendship. Jonathan, the current king of Israel's son, and David, one of the king's servants (who had been anointed by the Prophet as the next king of Israel), were immediately BFFs. The scripture says in 1 Samuel 18 that Jonathan and David's souls were knitted. Jonathan proved his faithfulness throughout his life by defying the king, his Father, to keep David safe. David endured several life threats from King Saul because of jealousy, but Jonathan warned David each time. Jonathan did not worry about his position as the prince. He was not concerned about himself because he loved David as himself.

I would argue there is no stronger application of friendship and faithfulness to it in scripture besides Jesus himself. Faithfulness can appear in very practical seemingly insignificant ways, but these are the keys to identifying this characteristic of the Spirit's fruit. First, you want to look for someone who keeps their Word not only to you, their friend, sister, cousin but also when it is difficult and inconvenient. We tend to look at those who have always been there for us, but what about when their aging grandparents need them to mow the lawn or the volunteering at church keeps you from scheduling coffee with the new hottie at the office? This is the time when our faith FULL ness is tested. Nothing is wrong with going out to have fun, but it is imperative that you have someone who is committed to a greater purpose than themselves. Faith allows us to believe that the Lord's will is better than the plan we envisioned.

Fellas: At this point, I hope you have been faithful to a few things. Faithful to your relationship with God, your fiancé, church, family, career, etc. These areas show up in your life, and so does the effort, time, and attention you give each area. You will want to look for a friend who you can clearly see this characteristic in his life. You will want to witness him balance his responsibilities and not be running all over town because he has overcommitted.

You want to make sure the man you select for this characteristic is good at time management and boundaries so that he can be present with you. A man who walks in faithfulness is more than a present body; he is a willing vessel while he is present. You will want to look for the guy who might volunteer in the thankless positions. These are extremely important positions, but no one is praising how great the chair setup is. This is the man who might be a little more in the background, but somehow, he is always there at the right time. This may be a mentor, older brother, or disciple in your life. Someone who has shown you that, over time, you are *valuable. Someone who has intentionality to set and keep plans with you.*

Ladies: We can have some friends who are faithful to a fault. Sometimes we have those friends who will literally fight for us even though they KNOW we're wrong. This is NOT the kind of loyal friendship I am referring to. We all need to be corrected every now and then. I am talking about the friend who will keep you accountable to volunteer or go to the gym with you even when you put up a fight (like me). You want to see consistency in her prayer and devotional life. You want to see her show up and participate in small group. You will want a woman who can manage her schedule and still make time for others.

This woman will be dependable throughout the wedding process to help make sure things stay on track. She will also have the character to remain in the commitment area, where you hopefully ask the group to join you in prayer over your marriage. This woman will take the time to really think about the commitment piece and give an honest answer. A faithful friend will diligently tear down unhealthy walls in your life. They will walk you through the process. Not to be your Savior or a crutch but to be your comfort and an encourager. A woman who is faithful to challenge you in growth is such an important quality to have in life, let alone one of the most important decisions in your life. This reminds me of the scripture, *"Better is open rebuke than hidden love. Faithful are the wounds of a friend; profuse are the kisses of an enemy."* (Proverbs 27:5-6, ESV)

These wounds are not intentional nor are they meant to harm you. Much like exercise it is a practice in stretching you to your best capacity. This is obviously a friend who has spent time and added value much more than they have taken withdrawals from the relationship. This is a special bond because the relational equity must be built up over time.

This woman will be a blessing to your life more than you know you need. The grace and comfort that she walks in will show you how important you are to your Heavenly Father. The Lord talks about His *"...steadfast love is great to the Heavens, your faithfulness to the clouds."* *(Psalm 57:10, ESV)* She is an example of the consistency of our God. Of course, she is human and cannot be your God, but you will notice her God-given ability to show up when others have failed. As you are looking for this lady, make sure that you gain this characteristic of the fruit of the Spirit in order to show up for her and your husband-to-be.

Let Him Read This

Hats off to the groom.

Alright, time to give the book to your fiancé. No, seriously, stop reading this right now, give the book to him, and make sure he reads this chapter. Not only for his sake but for yours. Hello sir. It's nice to meet you. Your beautiful bride-to-be has been reading this book about praying for your marriage and choosing your wedding party. Not because something is wrong but in preparation for your lives together. You will want to look at a few other chapters after finishing this one.

You're the groom and you took a massive step when you asked her out when you went to that show or played that game. You took bigger steps when you started to eat differently, dress differently, or maybe you had it all together; this is you we're talking about! You took greater steps when you met her crew, knew she was 'the one', bought the ring, and asked her to be your wife. So I want to thank you for being **bold**. Thank you for being courageous, kind, compassionate, caring, and most of all, willing to be a covering.

What is a covering? Some would describe a covering as something or someone who covers and protects, someone who guards. You are taking on a huge task to cover your wife so let me say thank you! I assume you've thought about this in the natural, but I want to shed a little light on what that looks like spiritually. Naturally, you can show up as a provider, a protector, or an actual jacket when she said she wouldn't get cold (but did). Spiritually you have agreed to be Christ on Earth in this scenario. Christ is the bridegroom of the church. He prays for the church and loves the church.

He sacrificed for the church; He even died for the church. Using Ephesians 5:25-33 as the example, you are to show these characteristics and actions to your wife. I don't think you need to go actively seeking a life-or-death situation, but you are to place her life, safety, and protection above your own if the time comes.

You are to wash your wife with the water of the Word of God. This means it's your responsibility to know the Word and to wash/speak the Word over her. Speaking the Word of God not only builds her up, it also is a reminder of positioning in the relationship. If you are consistently speaking life over her she will receive and multiply the word seeds spoken. The opposite is also true. You may not always have many words but the Scripture is full of wisdom, instruction, counsel, and encouragement. Rehearsing the Word over your wife is cleansing to the soul and life-giving to her very core.

I wanted to speak to you about this in case it was overlooked and not explained. The way a husband shows his love for his wife has a spiritual aspect that requires more than her submission. She is to follow you as you follow after Christ. It's a lot easier to do when she knows you are actively seeking the Lord and speaking the Word of God over her. Your relationship with Christ is apparent in the way you treat her. I want to encourage you to develop a prayer life if you don't already have one. This is simply the discipline to communicate with the Lord and to allow space and time for Him to communicate with you. You might hear His voice audibly, through a feeling or strong sense that repeats. He might speak to you in dreams, other people or most commonly through the Bible.

What does an active prayer life look like? Daily, if not moment by-moment, communication with God. It does not have to look or sound fancy. It should be genuine and not selfish. You should be asking the Lord what He wants and praying for the needs of others as well as yourself. You are His son and He wants to hear from you, to speak to you. As the priest and leader of your home, you will want clear vision from the Lord. Having this direction will show you where you should be going, and the preparation needed to achieve His perfect will for your life and the lives of those you lead.

"Where there is no prophetic vision, the people cast off restraint, but blessed is he who keeps the law." (Proverbs 29:18, ESV)

Ensure you are leading your family to the place the Lord has called you to. This would be hard to know if you have barely spent time with Him. Just like you desire to spend time with your fiancé to get to know her and how she thinks, you will need to do the same thing with the Lord so that you can grow in your relationship with Him. This is so important because your family's success and marriage depends on your communication with the Lord.

One of the ways to set your prayer life on fire is to be baptized into Holy Spirit. I want to point out that this is different from receiving salvation. I would also like to reaffirm that YOU HAVE HOLY SPIRIT living inside you if you have accepted Christ. You are literally a temple and Holy Spirit's dwelling place. As believers, we have access to walk in the power to heal, to do miracles, signs and wonders because we have Holy Spirit. Being baptized in the Holy Spirit allows us to have Him living in us and be completely submerged in Him. Jesus was raised from the dead because of the power of Holy Spirit.

"You, however, are not in the flesh but in the Spirit, if in fact, the Spirit of God dwells in you. Anyone who does not have the Spirit of Christ does not belong to Him. But if Christ is in you, although the body is dead because of sin, the Spirit is life because of righteousness. If the Spirit of Him who raised Jesus from the dead dwells in you, He who raised Christ Jesus from the dead will also give life to your mortal bodies through His Spirit who dwells in you." (Romans 8:9-11, ESV)

The Word also says we will do greater works than Jesus. This is because we are empowered by Holy Spirit.

Why is being baptized in the Holy Spirit important? You are able to pray the will of the Father led by the Holy Spirit. You can receive the evidence of praying in tongues which is the Spirit praying through your mouth the things you may not even be thinking about. This is an advantage because you may not know what is coming, but the Lord does.

Whether you pray in English, your native language, or tongues the main thing is that the power of the Holy Spirit ignites your prayer life. The Holy Spirit also gives you the power to do the will of the Father. You can only achieve the God-sized plans through Him not in your own strength. The Word says,

"Therefore, one who speaks in a tongue should pray that he may interpret. For if I pray in a tongue, my spirit prays, but my mind is unfruitful. What am I to do? I will pray with my spirit, but I will pray with my mind also; I will sing praise with my spirit, but I will sing with my mind also." (1 Corinthians 14:13-15, ESV)

You want to seek the favor of the Lord for your life and your wife. I encourage you to remain in constant submission to the will of Jesus because you are, in fact, His bride. You are learning from the best, so you can remain in sync with his plan when your connection to Christ is uninterrupted. Developing a relationship with the Lord will require similar actions but is unique to each of us. You may be a laying prostrate prophetic prayer warrior who sits with the Lord for hours a day. That is great if you have that kind of setup. Some of us simply get quiet before Him and read scripture aloud because we're too exhausted to think.

You might be doing a reading plan with some buddies because you need accountability and want to discuss the Word of God with your peers. Ask Him to enter the mundane and the awesome aspects of your life. You will want to increase your prayer life because you are becoming a priest in your own right. The Word of God informs us that we are royalty. We are kings and priests but that comes with the responsibility of protection. I suggest that having her back in the spirit is infinitely more important than the natural. When you cover her in the spirit, you know the things that are coming in the natural.

You can see, address and completely obliterate problems before they arise. Your words hold weight. Your words hold power. (The power of life and death is in the tongue; Proverbs 18:20-22). Just as the importance of the Father's voice to his children, the Word of God in the mouth of the man you love is comforting and strengthening. You have the ability to be a prayer covering and protection for the most important person in your life, your wife.

Part of your preparation as a prayer covering for your wife is simply knowing the Word of God. You cannot draw from a source you are not connected to. You need to be connected to the Word of God for yourself. You also need to have the seeds of God's Word buried in your heart so that at its proper time, the Word will grow and sprout out of your mouth when you need it most. John 14:25 says the Holy Spirit will teach you all things and bring to your memory all He said to us.

You are the one bearing the seeds of life for your future, both naturally and spiritually. In moments of joy, you need the Word to rejoice; in moments of laughter, you need to know that your laughter is healing to your bones; in moments of conflict, you need the direction to bring your ought to your wife and to have spiritual authority involved if you cannot settle the dispute. You need to know what wisdom to give her when she asks for your opinion or solution.

You need to be the mirror of the Word to her, so she is sanctified with each encounter with you. You need to know the Words of your Heavenly Father to know that you make the coffee! Okay, maybe that one is not biblical, but I've never read the book of Shebrews. Bad dad joke, I know. You need to be versed in this love letter to remind you to always be intoxicated by the love of your wife and her body. Can I get an amen?

You don't know how to lean on these scriptures without knowing God's Word. You can't leave cheesy Christian pickup lines around the house from the Song of Solomon if you've never read it! If you don't already, immerse yourself in the Word of God daily. If you already do, it's time for double dipping. That beautiful gift you are engaged to will need to pull from a well and you can store up that good good. You can be the brook bubbling over with compassion, patience, grace, knowledge, and wisdom, most importantly with love.

Now that we understand the spiritual covering, you need support! I'm talking; you know you cannot bench press that much support. I'm talking; you better not go out on that field without your helmet and your children's helmet support. I'm talking; have your wingman get this woman's number support. You need men who understand this kind of support to stand with you.

In the midst of hormones, in the midst of her asking questions during the Super Bowl, or in the midst of her asking if you prefer sea foam, teal, or turquoise ribbons for the party favors support. You need men who will encourage and invigorate your love for your King Jesus and ignite your king qualities! Men who will drive you to the bosom of your wife and not the bottle. Men who will protect your eye gates from the devastating effects of pornography or incredible violence. You need brothers who will challenge you to keep growing. Friends who will lay down their life for you as an example for you to lay down your life for your wife.

Do you have these types of friends? Do you have relationships that press you into fine wine? Men, who demand your very best all the while encouraging you by letting you know you're more than enough before you step foot on the journey? These types of men need to be in the wedding and on the marriage journey. I want you to be mindful of the company you keep in this season. The Word of God says *bad company corrupts good morals. (1 Corinthians 15:33)* You will want to search for these connections and highlight the ones that bear the Fruit of the Spirit.

This is not the time to be listening to the guy who is always clowning you about marriage being the end of your life or the buddy who is always suggesting movies that send you home struggling in your mind. This is the time to reach out to those mentors, the big brothers, your spiritual Fathers who will speak peace, truth, purity and wisdom to your spirit man. You need him to get beefed up in the spirit because sanctification is coming. Prayer will not necessarily eliminate all your marriage's hardships but will cause you to respond to them differently. I have never met a woman complaining that her spouse prayed too much.

Now, this is a message to you on the Pharisee praying level. Once you hear from the Lord, go share with your wife. Wash your face, brush your teeth, and invite her into the secret place with you! You are not just praying to pray. You are communicating with your Heavenly Father about the things that concern you, the things that bring you joy, and the things He is working on. You get to share intimacy with your wife once you've been with the Lord. Your pursuit of Jesus will ignite her pursuit of Jesus.

When you reach out to your bros, your crew, ensure they can carry this load with you. Make sure these men are not just willing but able. Don't just get matching socks and converse so you can look cool. Don't be dressed to the nines without help in this battle. Invite men who will hold you to the standard of the Word of God. You will not regret taking this seriously. These men become your sounding board when she drives you up the wall. When you just need to get away and play ball.

The men you surround yourself with will be the men who have your ear and are ultimately the ones who will plant seeds of love, faith, and unity or discord. The men you are in relationship with will determine your commitment to Christ and His daughter. Please be intentional about the personalities, habits, language, and media you expose yourself to. Please have fun but do not have fun at the expense of your relationship with the creator or your bride.

More Than a Day

Commitment

There is a commitment beyond the day of the wedding. I encourage you to ask your bridesmaids and the maid of honor to join you for more than just the wedding day. Preparation for the wedding day is important, but the enemy attacks even more after you say I do. I am sure you have heard of stories where people lived together for years, and their relationship was great. The couple hardly argued, maybe even had children together, but as soon as they decided to join together in covenant, they had problems they had never experienced before. (I believe it is outside of the Lord's will to be physically intimate before the covenant commitment of marriage.) Those 'problems' are not a coincidence; it's intentional.

That said, I think it would be a wonderful goal to keep your marriage covered in prayer. Who better to join you on that journey than the men and women who covered you physically and spiritually from the very beginning?

Commitment not only means taking your time to pray for this couple and one another, but it also requires sacrifice. Some things require a greater level of preparation. One of the spiritual disciplines that the church seemed to cast aside is fasting. We know that fasting enlarges our capacity to carry spiritual things and endues us with power through the Holy Spirit. I encourage you to make sure that the people you choose to cover you and your fiancé can tap into this discipline on your behalf.

There are times the Word of God directs us to fast as a group. You might know it as a corporate fast. This is the act of a group coming together to fast and pray for a specific purpose. This scripture is an example of a group coming together to send two individuals out on purpose. *"While they were worshiping the Lord and fasting, the Holy Spirit said, "Set apart for me Barnabas and Saul for the work to which I have called them." Then after fasting and praying, they laid their hands on them and sent them off."* Acts 13:2-3 ESV. Not only do we see the laying on of hands, but worship and fasting. This should be a part of the wedding planning process as well as some time set aside after the I do. Imagine if once a year we did not just celebrate the completion of another year together, but the wedding warriors (as many who were able) gathered together to fast, worship and lay hands on the couple sending them into purpose with prayer?

How powerful a display of Godly community! I want you and your fiancé to think, pray and discuss the importance and rate of this marriage fellowship that is right for you. You want to go into the planning process knowing your plan and expectation for your wedding party. This part of the process needs some serious thought and attention because it is weightier than the decorations. It is weightier than the entertainment or even the honeymoon location. All the natural things can be in place, but if we miss the major spiritual preparation, how effective are decorations at keeping your marriage healthy? I want to stress the importance of being extravagant in your spiritual preparation, which means inviting people into the space with you.

The preparation is more than a quick hey God every now and then. It's more like realizing your inability to succeed in any area of your life, let alone becoming one with another imperfect human being and asking the

Lord to step in. You are asking the perfect bridegroom to come into every aspect of your marriage and prep the areas of your heart the way that only He can. Having your team, circle, and wedding warriors join you is one of the most powerful ways you build your foundation of marriage.

I'm reminded of two scriptures *"Truly, I say to you, whatever you bind on Earth shall be bound in Heaven, and whatever you loose on Earth shall be loosed in Heaven. Again I say to you, if two of you agree on Earth about anything they ask, it will be done for them by my Father in Heaven. For where two or three are gathered in my name, there am I among them.""* Matthew 18:18-20 ESV and *"And though a man might prevail against one who is alone, two will withstand him—a threefold cord is not quickly broken."* Ecclesiastes 4:12 ESV. These scriptures remind us that we are stronger together. We can try to take on this new journey alone but the strength of our prayer and fasting is exponentially more powerful when we are gathered in the name of the Lord. What does it mean to have God in the midst? We are changed in the midst of the Lord. He can refresh and renew us. The presence of God calls us into a deeper place of intimacy and inner healing. He is the one who calms the storm. He is the one who heals, delivers, and sets free. I desire His presence to change me and mold me. Hopefully, you will too.

The specifics may look different for everyone, but I would suggest that regular scheduled prayer and fasting be implemented. You may feel it's too much to ask the whole wedding party, but I would ask my maid (or matron) of honor and best man to join you in a lifetime of coverage. It sounds like insurance. This is not to say that you meet weekly to cover your marriage or that you all have to be in the same place, but I think it would be beneficial to pray and fast quarterly for the strength, longevity, joy, peace, and prosperity of your marriage.

I encourage you and your fiancé to pray and discuss the people you are comfortable with covering your marriage. You want to make sure that it is someone who is mature spiritually and someone you both trust.

You really want your spouse to be comfortable with the people you are expecting to cover you and potentially see into sensitive places of each of your lives. This is not the space for your friend who likes to pray gossip. I know it's a terrible concept, but we have people that will pray about your business publicly when it is meant to be protected. This is such a place of honor and intimate fellowship to be invited into. We must learn how to create safe places in the secret place for others, especially regarding intercession.

Intercession is a type of prayer where you become the person standing in the gap for another. When someone becomes the go between, they gain access to things and information they may not otherwise require. A wedding warrior should be expected to protect the secrets of the battle plan and the weak spots in your platoon. You should not need to worry about people exposing the intimate details of your relationship, plans, or marriage. The wedding party should be there to bolster the places where you know there is a lack. The wedding warriors are a prayer shield to protect you from the enemy's fiery darts. Your wedding party will not tweet or text about everything; they'll pray. You will want to keep certain areas of communication to a minimum so that the enemy does not get a whiff of any weaknesses.

Sometimes we are not as focused on the battles in the spirit realm, which is why you need backup. Planning your wedding can be a time when you forget to prioritize your quiet time with the Lord, or you fill your schedule to the brim because of the deadline. This is why you need a Godly community reminding you of the main thing. If I have not been clear, that main thing is Jesus. Jesus is the focus, ultimately. Your marriage is to glorify Him, and your support system will lead you back to that conclusion if you choose wisely.

Being a wedding warrior will require commitment. Obviously, more than the one day or the days leading up to that day. Prayer and intercession do not require a trumpet or announcement. This assignment, if you choose to accept it, is a covert mission that has to continue to be maintained. Bride and groom, you will need to be open and honest about this commitment from the beginning to clearly define your expectations and give time to see if they are up for the task. The person will need to seek the LORD to see if they have the time, bandwidth, and spiritual maturity to keep you covered.

You also have a commitment to your wedding warriors. If they have accepted your terms of engagement, you are submitting yourself and your heart to their words. You are asking for their wisdom and counsel, especially when you do not want to hear it. I often make the joke that I do not like my friends when they instruct me to do something I do not want to do. Sometimes I know they are correct, but I do not want to put the work in to do what they are telling me. I can find myself in a place of submission to them even when it's hard. I truly desire to grow, but change is required for growth. Speaking with a friend earlier today, I reminded her that we all have different gifts and abilities. I may operate in wisdom, and she operates in knowledge, but both gifts are required to fully realize what the Lord has for the body at that moment. We are one body as Believers with different positions and responsibilities. We cannot all be eyes or arms.

We need diversity to cover our blind spots. So if you desire to be covered, you must be willing to be corrected in LOVE. You must be willing to hear that you need to apologize. *"Whoever heeds instruction is on the path to life, but he who rejects reproof leads others astray."* Proverbs 10:17 ESV This is why your decision to select your wedding warrior crew is so important. You need these people to actively be a personal Bible to your relationship. Another scripture comes to mind *"for by wise guidance you can wage your war, and in abundance of counselors there is victory."* Proverbs 24:6 ESV There is success when we have wise guidance. If marriage is attacked as if it were a battle, you need those counselors around you to give wise and biblical advice.

There are a few areas that I assume people have under control. I assumed that most women have purity under control and that the fight is over once you're engaged because you can see the light at the end of the tunnel. Unfortunately, I have been informed otherwise. Our society has done a great job of blurring the lines of what is acceptable before marriage. During the engagement, people who have great intentions fall into sexual immorality, and I believe purity is one of the things that seal the covenant. So why not pray against this temptation? Why not serve as accountability partners to help safeguard the marriage against something proven to weaken the bond of that lifelong relationship?

As a friend and fellow sister in Christ, I want to do everything I can to protect the covenant. So how do we accomplish that? First, we need to identify the fruit and spiritual strengths. Know who you'd like to be responsible for taking each role. There may be more or less roles according to your specific party. Here are a few positions that need to be filled or highlighted. Some you may want to share directly, and some you may read and want to relay.

You will need to identify your strategist for both the groomsmen and the bridesmaids. There will most undoubtedly be a forerunner for this position. Some men and women can pray the shingles off a roof and cancer off the Earth but may not have the best organization skills. This task assumes that you've prayed with each of your wedding warriors. Prayer amongst friends is not as common as we'd think. I would ask a friend to pray for me if they happened to be there in time of emergency but not just to seek the Lord together. This is potentially why some Christians don't pray for each other's marriages and more so for the preparation. We have not established a lifestyle of prayer as a community, and it shows.

Hopefully, you and your strategist see the need to join in prayer when things are well. Praying after an emergency or problem arises is reactionary. The Bible commands us to *pray without ceasing.* (1

Thessalonians 5:17) I see some people who do well at this personally but not as a community.

Your strategist will be excited at the thought that you are intentionally weaving prayer into your wedding planner. Hopefully, this person will already be close enough to you and your fiancé to know some of the personal areas of your life that may need more attention than others. Your strategist can be your maid/matron of honor, but this person needs to be involved. Your strategist will need strong discernment to provide specific prayer points for you and your spouse, and the rest of the wedding party. Your strategist will also be the one to call a moment of prayer when needed throughout the wedding planning. Select this person on the evidence of an active prayer life. A prayer life that you have seen change some things in the Earth. If you believe this person is not your best man or in the place of honor for the bridesmaids, please be careful to identify them so that your prayer time is regularly implemented before the wedding and if you decide to ask others to join you after the wedding.

Maid/Matron of Honor

There are so many things that come to mind when I think about this title. Early one morning, while meditating on the LORD, I felt like the definition of this role is a woman who will remind you to honor Christ in your marriage. When I think about the word honor, majesty and elegance, come to mind, and these are both royal things. This is an extremely integral position in your tribe, posse, or military unit. As second in command, I trust this woman would help steer you in the right direction for fashion and faith. This particular role should be lifelong, intentional, and strategic. Select this woman based on her ability to speak the Word of God into your life and situation to ensure you remain in a state of honor and glorify the bridegroom of the church, Jesus Christ, and in your model covenant to the world.

How you decide to go about this request for commitment will be totally up to you. I know that this person is generally close to you. Hopefully, someone that you already pray with regularly. This person would typically take a strong role in creating a prayer schedule with the other ladies both with and without you. If this lady is not the planning type, ask her to partner with a more administrative person who loves doing this. The two will want to get together and outline the prayer points that stick out to them as led by Holy Spirit and come up with points outside of the suggested topics.

This person should not be brand new to covering you in prayer. She ideally would be the person who covers you when you are fasting. She potentially should be one of your accountability partners and someone you receive wisdom from. She will have your back and serve you naturally, but she is an integral piece of your relationship going forward. If she is a matron of honor, you will want to select a person with a marriage you admire and one that has exhibited the major markers of a Christian relationship.

You may want to ask for her advice, which should be steeped in scripture, not her opinion. Your honor position should not just honor you, but she should honor God, your covenant, your husband, your family, and the other bridesmaids. This is a special position of servanthood naturally and one that seeks to serve, not to be seen. Do not allow your loyalty to betray you in this decision. Do not allow the pressure of expectation to make this decision for you. You need a faithful and wise woman versed in the Word to fill this role.

Best Man

This role is to be the right hand to the groom, both naturally and spiritually. This position, much like the maid/matron of honor, will most likely be your strategist. I know it is difficult to get men together so he will need to be a person who can lead others to this desired relationship with prayer concerning your marriage. Your best man will encourage you to keep seeking the face of God during the wedding and after. You will want to select this man for his organization, memory, and ability to be detail-oriented, especially if you are not.

This man will hopefully be someone close to your heart, like a brother. Similar to the desired David and Jonathan relationship, where even though Jonathan was the next in line for the Kingdom, he served and protected David from the misguided anger of Saul. As a best man, I suggest that you ask for a lifelong commitment. You will want to clarify that you will need him beyond the wedding day. You will need him beyond the occasional call to blow off steam about her always being late or difficult. You will need your best man to give you sound biblical counsel and speak life over your covenant instead of referring to your wife as 'the ole ball and chain' or accusing you of being whipped when you've made a commitment with the love of your life.

Your commitment to your best man is to allow accountability, correction, and encouragement. We have a tendency to beat ourselves up when things are not going just so, or you've messed up in the same area. Instead of staying in that space allow your best man to pick you up from the place of heaviness. Your best man is to be one of your closest brothers in Christ. If he also happens to be your biological brother, awesome. Do not select your current roommate if you know he struggles to get to work on time. This is a place of responsibility and priesthood. Your best man should know the Word of God to build you up instead of jokingly tearing you down.

Parents of the Bride

I encourage you to pray for your daughter. You have prepared her for this moment, to grow in her faith walk and make sound decisions. This is not the time to be overbearing or instruct, in your opinion. This is a time to take your concerns to your Heavenly Father, who loves her more than you ever could. Pray into the spaces and places where you and your parents struggle in marriage or relationships. Pray to break those generational habits that are not Kingdom. Pray for the health and longevity of this union. We should consider Christ in the things that we share. We want to be open about testimonies that you've overcome to provide strength and clarity. If you see things lacking in their spirituality, the Bible says to restore them in a spirit of gentleness. Take the approach that this is not only your daughter but your sister in Christ. We will take a different tone when coming from a place of intentionality and grace. We know the areas that have tied us up in the past.

Mom, be encouraging and full of peace for your daughter. Remember, she hears you in her head and knows your desires before you speak them. Remember to prepare your heart spiritually for the wedding day, not just the moment you get to see your little princess come into her womanhood and purpose for her life. Be a Naomi allowing Holy Spirit to give you counsel and direction on what to say and the timing. Things will be different than they were for you. That is okay because you are two different people. Make sure that you are encouraging relationship over the wedding. The relationship over your hopes for their future. Be the prayer covering you've (hopefully) always been to your daughter, praying over her safety, joy, peace, growth, etc. Become her prayer partner not the naysayer in her life. Allow the relationship to change and be the wisdom she can lean into.

Dad, I cannot imagine what it means to let your daughter grow to this stage of life. I hope you feel at peace and trust the man who will be stepping in to be her covering. This is a period of time where you can reassure her that you are there for her and that anything she needs, in your power to do so, is there. However, there should be a shift and transfer in how you cover your daughter. The idea of leaving and cleaving is an instruction for you too. Become a prayer partner for the things that concern you about their relationship. You are needed, but you must realize she has been given another covering.

I encourage you not to worry but to pray. You are her foundation, but she must begin to build a new foundation. Encourage her to trust him as she trusts you. Encourage him that he is capable of leading his family as well as building a strong covering for her. Let him in on the things that you have grown in over the years. Most of all, be praying and speaking to the success and longevity of their marriage, not how much better you have been able to provide and protect her.

Parents of the Groom

This is such an exciting time to see your son step into a greater level of commitment, responsibility, and joy. By now you have seen how he has begun to change his habits, change his posture from being taken care of to taking care. You have watched him grow and fall, but this is one area when the Bible is very clear that he is to leave you and cleave to his wife. Now, this may seem dramatic, maybe even rude, but I want to encourage you that you have prepared him for this moment. This moment is not just I DO; this moment is servanthood. This is where he can cook a few meals while his wife is out of town so he and the kiddos can survive. This moment is him outdoing a God-fearing woman in showing honor and mutual submission. You've taught him to love and to lead. You've taught him to grow and to be independent. (If not, take this time to pray about those things for your son) There is still time to cover him in prayer.

Mom, I hope you are preparing your heart for your son to have another woman fill his heart. You birthed, raised, and fought for and with him to be the man you see today. When you miss his presence, tell the Lord. Do not force your hand for quality time or attention. He is being obedient to the scriptures *"But from the beginning of creation, 'God made them male and female.' 'Therefore a man shall leave his Father and mother and hold fast to his wife, and the two shall become one flesh.' So they are no longer two but one flesh. What therefore God has joined together, let not man separate."* Mark 10:6-9 ESV Do your best to help him follow this Word. This does not mean you stop praying or caring for your son, but one of the best ways to support him is to pray for their health. Pray for the generational hang-ups that your family may have dealt with. Pray for their love to grow more in Christ and with one another. You have seen relationships and how fragile they can be. Speak life over your daughter and their unity.

Dad, thank you for being there. If you weren't there the entire time, you are here now, and that means something. I hope you have a true prayer relationship with the Lord Jesus. This is your opportunity to show your son by example what it means to be a biblical covering for his wife. You can direct him right back to the throne of grace every time he looks to you for advice. You have the opportunity to warn about the pitfalls and rejoice in the triumphs you've had. Be connected to the Lord in such a way that your communication is so close to the Word of God that he remembers to wash his bride in the water of the Word. Encourage him to be the best parts of you, especially the picture of Jesus, the bridegroom, and the church. Your voice holds weight. Ensure you are speaking the Word and praying for their success.

Friends

Please encourage your friends whether they are in the wedding or not, to pray for your wedding as well as the God-ordained will for your marriage. Ask them to be the ones to gather around you in a posture of prayer for the purpose and perfect will for your marriage. You and your spouse will need encouragement, words of life, and reminders that this covenant relationship is about more than the two of you being in love. You need to remember that you are giving the enemy a black eye when you wake up and serve others in private and public. Friends, true friends, do not need every detail of your life to take action to pray for you as an individual and as a couple. I hope you will encourage your friend group to pray for you beyond your wedding day. Even if it's not a collective thing, having consistent Holy Spirit led prayer concerning your covenant should be a part of a Christian community BEFORE there is turbulence or hardship.

Flight crews do not ignore the flight safety procedures because it is beautiful weather. They ensure passengers are wearing their seatbelts and only moving about the cabin according to the safety protocols. If it is pouring rain or inclement weather, it makes sense to follow their directions, but they know we could experience turbulence at any moment. If we trust that the Bible gives us the safety procedures for life, we should not ignore scriptures that tell us to bear one another's burdens. We should be preparing our circle for success. We can pray for our friends in any season and truly expect results. The Word says, *"Is anyone among you suffering? Let him pray. Is anyone cheerful? Let him sing praise. Is anyone among you sick? Let him call for the Elders of the church, and let them pray over him, anointing him with oil in the name of the Lord. And the prayer of faith will save the one who is sick, and the Lord will raise him up. And if he has committed sins, he will be forgiven. Therefore, confess your sins to one another and pray for one another, that you may be healed. The prayer of a righteous person has great power as it is working."* James 5:13-16 ESV

Family

I would specifically ask my family to pray for the wedding process and beyond. Your life will be intertwined with these people throughout your marriage as they are family. Even if you only see them on the holidays, family is a vital point of your faith community because you will most likely be engaged with them at some level for the rest of your life. This may not be a group you often get together to hang out with, but if there is a possibility, take advantage. Family typically understands your personality better than other people in your life until this point. They know your history. Your past mistakes as well as your victories.

Although family can be overbearing or sometimes non-existent, they tend to care for you. I would ask my family to pray and even fast together once before the wedding. This will be a bonding moment for the family whether they have a role in the ceremony or not. Your family has a specific relationship with you that others will not understand, so their prayers will be different. You know what to expect from your family, but you can use this as an invitation to grow deeper in the Lord together. I promise this is not an opportunity you want to miss out on. What if your marriage is the moment that some of the most important people in your life walk into a relationship with Christ for the first time or on a deeper level because you handed them the opportunity to care for you in this way? What a powerful witness!

In my personal experience, my family has grown at different rates, and everyone is not called to grow the same. The Lord has a specific relationship with each of us, but your family has often set your spiritual foundation. Even the way you see and experience God can be affected by this group of people. Drawing your family into this spiritual space with you is an honor. They may not all come, and that might sting, but the ones who commit will deepen not only your biological connection but your spiritual one. Cherish the opportunity to share this moment more than the photo opp on your wedding day. Please, by all means, take the shot but make it bigger than a moment. Make it a lifestyle.

Church Family

With all the excitement of the engagement and wedding, I encourage you to commission your church family to PRAY and FAST for you! This may seem really obvious, but it is not always our go to even as believers. We get swept up in the moment, especially if it has been a long time coming. As a result, we can overlook some of the normal practices we put in place to walk out our lives in a manner pleasing to God. *"I, therefore, a prisoner for the Lord, urge you to walk in a manner worthy of the calling to which you have been called, with all humility and gentleness, with patience, bearing with one another in love, eager to maintain the unity of the Spirit in the bond of peace."* Ephesians 4:1-3 ESV. Per this scripture, we must maintain unity and bear one another up.

This decision is life-altering, and I urge that your small group or after Sunday service brunch crew should be invited into this moment of spiritual prep for your marriage. Everyone may not make it to the wedding list, but if you share community, Bible study fellowship, or breaking bread, ask these folks to seek the Lord on your behalf. You would typically ask your small group or church community to pray if something was wrong. Why not ask them to pray for your new life with another human being? We want to remember to be proactive, not reactive. These people already have a relationship with you in a biblical context. Give them the responsibility to partner in prayer. Be honored when they join you as they see fit to make you a priority.

It may be until the wedding day or as Holy Spirit leads, but this is still an amazing display of unity. We know that where there is unity, the Lord COMMANDS His blessing. Let those you already trust and have a relationship with into this commitment. There are levels to how much information you give access to, but in the long run, if you have groups already functioning in this capacity, it makes sense for them to show up for this part as well.

Clergy

Most people have not stayed under the same pastoral covering their whole lives. Even if you have attended the same church, you may have had different leaders preaching and teaching the Word of God to you. I know I had two different children's leaders, another minister for my teen years, a church change with a new pastor, and young adult ministers that probably knew me better than the Pastor. I have spent the majority of my life at two churches: one for eighteen years and the other for about ten years. I have cultivated relationships with ministers, mentors, and pastors who have walked me through different seasons and stages of life.

This is more than asking your current Pastor, whether you know them well or not, to do your marriage counseling and pray for you. This is gathering your counselors, teachers of wisdom, Word, and might to seek the Lord's face concerning you. They may not know one another or even pray together, but the invitation to this group of people may be something you would like to choose. What if your save the dates had an invitation to pray and fast for your union?

How can we change this cultural narrative to grow a community of faith for more than the wedding ceremony? I know that all these invitations to seek Heaven on your fiancé and your behalf might sound extreme, but what better way to shield your union from the attacks of the enemy than to literally and spiritually have an army of prayer warriors covering you? I know the ministers in your life may be busy or live out of town, but what a testament to how much their spiritual covering meant in your life in the past that you would invite them into this decision as well.

Maybe this looks like a 15-minute prayer call. Perhaps it looks like an hour Zoom or a dinner filled with fun, laughter, and wisdom. You know your people. If you believe they may be too busy, let them be the ones to say I am not available to commit. You must make it known that you would like spiritual support.

Covering the Wedding Party Prayers

Vision

Father, we thank you for encouraging us to get a vision from you. Thank you for giving us clarity. We ask that you give us vision for our marriage. Lord would you show us how to live as a true son and daughter. Reveal to us our specific individual and collective assignments as we walk through life together. Father, would you show us your heart for ourselves and each other. Lord, give us your perspective on your child, my spouse. I ask that You would communicate your perfect will for us in such a way that we can both understand, receive and walk out. Lord, when my spouse is weak in faith, help me to be strong so that the word you spoke will be our clear focus and desire. Please show us your purpose for being in covenant and direct us on the steps needed to fulfill your will. We ask for strategy to become the couple you've designed and destined us to be. Lord, we thank you for showing us how our gifts, talents, and abilities align to achieve the call on our marriage. Jesus, help us be open and honest about the desires you've placed in our hearts before while and after saying 'I do'. Father let our answer always be yes to you. Lord, we ask that you give us the steps and resources to be all that you've called us to be. Help us to consistently come to you for direction, clarity and strategy over the life of our relationship. In Jesus name, amen

Leadership

Jesus thank you for being the great Shepherd. Lord we know that your Word tells us not to learn on our own understanding but in all of our ways to acknowledge you and you would make straight our paths. Jesus, right now we humble ourselves. Lord, we do not want to be humbled by you but we choose to acknowledge you as Lord. Holy Spirit you have the sit down and shut up card in our lives both individually and collectively. Lord, we submit to your leadership fist and foremost. God we recognize our frailty and weakness as flesh. Your word says that in our weakness your strength is made perfect. We want that perfect strength at the forefront of our marriage. God we thank you for your desire to lead us in your most perfect way. Jesus we thank you for coming to give us the perfect example of a life poured out. Holy Spirit as our guide we trust you and ask that you remind our heart to follow your lead. Father forgive us in advance when our impatience and worldly knowledge puffs us up. Help us to remember that we are but clay in the Master's hands. Jesus, thank You for being the head of the church and our high priest. Lord we are honored that we get to be your glory.

Lord, help us to allow you to have the final say. Let us always revere Your word above counsel, opinion or our preference. Jesus as the husband and priest of this family, I commit to submit to you and your way. I do not want to move without you. Lord as the wife and favor of this family I ask for the courage, trust and faith to submit to my husband especially when we disagree. Lord, help me to trust Holy Spirit in my husband. Lord Jesus, would you allow us to support and encourage one another in the areas where you have gifted us. Lord let us lead as unto You. Father let our aim always be to please you not to get our own way. Lord where you lead us we will go. What you lead us to do we will joyfully obey. When we are unsure let us always focus on you, the author, perfector and finisher of our faith. To you be all glory. In Jesus name, amen.

Glorifying God

Lord, I thank you that marriage is a sanctification process. Father, I ask that you help me outdo my spouse in showing honor. Thank you for giving me the privilege to be in communion with you and your child. Lord, help me to speak with honor, gentleness, and humility every time I speak to one of your children, especially my spouse. Father, I thank you for giving me a heart like yours. Lord, let me see them the way you do. Lord, your Word says, *"Love bears all things, believes all things, hopes all things, endures all things."* 1 Corinthians 13:7 ESV. Father, help me to believe the best about my spouse and their intentions. Lord, I trust your relationship with my spouse is leading and guiding them in your perfect will. I thank you for giving us the opportunity to give you glory in our relationship and show your glory through our relationship. Help us seek your perfect will and display goodness in Jesus's name, Amen.

Provision

Father, I know that you are the great provider, Jehovah Jireh. I thank you that you are El Shaddai, the all-sufficient one. I trust that in every season, we will be provided for. Lord, I thank you for times of abundance, and I thank you that if there is a season of want, all our needs will be provided according to your riches in glory. (Philippians 4:19) Lord, I thank you for hearing us when we cry out to you. I thank you that all we need to do is cry out to you, and you will deliver us out of all our troubles (Psalm 34:17). Lord, I thank you that in every season, we will learn to be content. Lord, help us to draw nearer to you in times of affliction, and help us to draw closer to each other. I thank you that two are better than one. (Ecclesiastes 4:9) Help us to come to you both individually and collectively use the gifts and resources you have given us to walk through any tough time we may face. Lord, thank you for coming to give us life and life more abundantly. Father, in addition to resources, I ask for an abundance of peace, joy, unity, grace, and favor. Please help us to remember that your presence is greater than any resource because you are the **source**. Lord, we love you. We trust you and your plan/purpose for our life in Jesus' name. Amen

Bride for Husband Prayer

Lord Jesus, I thank you that you cause my husband to be the priest of our home after your example. Father, I thank you for being the perfect bridegroom and telling us in your Word that you lay down your life for your bride. Lord, I ask that you empower my husband to love me as you love the church and give himself up for me so that he might sanctify me, cleansing me with the water of the Word. Lord, show him that to love me is to love himself. Lord, I ask that you help me honor, submit and respect his spiritual leadership as the priest of our home. Father, show me how to encourage the priestly royalty that he is. Lord, I ask that you help me to magnify the God-like character in him and allow him to lead empowered by Holy Spirit. Lord, I ask that you help me trust his spiritual leadership, that he hears and obeys your guidance for our household. I ask that you help me to be consistent in covering his mind in prayer so he can communicate clearly with you. Lord, allow your perfect love to cover a multitude of sins. Thank you for the grace you've given me and the grace you will help me show.

Lord Jesus, I thank you for the power of Holy Spirit. I am so thankful you decided to come and dwell with us when we receive salvation. Holy Spirit, thank you for drawing me to Jesus and leading me to the Gospel's truth. Holy Spirit, I ask that you would transform my spouse and I by your power. Lord, let us both sow to the spirit and not the flesh. (Galatians 6:8) Lord, as we grow in our walk with you, help us to walk in the baptism of Holy Spirit. Help us to be empowered to walk out this Christ-follower's life with all the tools available to us. We thank you for the power availed to us. Help us not just tap into it but to *live* in it. Holy Spirit change us from the inside out. Help our hearts remain soft toward your leading.

God, I thank you for my marriage. Thank you for my husband. Lord, I thank you for his heart. I thank you for allowing us to partner with me to make our home a place of peace, love and restoration. Holy Spirit, I thank you for my husband's knowledge of Your word. I thank you that he operates in the spirit of wisdom, counsel, strength, meekness, might, and love. Lord Jesus, help him to operate in every gift that you have given him. I thank you for giving him prophetic insight. I thank you that he worships you in spirit and in truth. God, I thank you that I am covered by his intercession. Father I thank you that he was created to glorify you uniquely and that you will establish in every way guiding him to the spaces and places of destiny. Holy Father I thank you for his patience to wait with you and for me. Holy Spirit, thank you for giving us Your timing and understanding. Lord, I declare that my marriage would be marked and overflowing with love, joy, laughter, love that I understand, rich conversation, fun, connection, understanding peace and growth. Jesus, help us to be healthy emotionally, physically, spiritually and mentally. I plead the blood of Jesus over my husband's mind. I thank you for peace that passes all understanding to guard his heart and mind. Will you remove any worry from his heart and body. Holy Spirit I ask that you would open up every door that you want him to walk through and send the provision in the direction you want him to walk. Lord you said that the steps of a good man are ordered by You. Help him to hear and see you clearly. Father, help me to love your son the way he deserves. Help me to respect him the way he desires in Jesus name, Amen.

Helpmeet

Father, we thank you that your daughter was created to be a helpmeet. Lord, we thank you for allowing us to be your bride before allowing us to be chosen by man. Lord, I thank you for teaching her to be your bride in her relationship with you. Lord, I thank you that your relationship with her has taught her to follow your vision and spread your gospel worldwide. Lord, in an area where it is easy to trust you and follow your lead but not as easy to follow man, would you empower her to trust the leading of the Holy Spirit in her husband. Lord make me a man worthy of following as I submit to you.

Lord Jesus, I ask you to show her how to strengthen and support his vision for the household and family. Would you show her how to cover her husband in prayer, which would help her be the helpmeet that he needs to walk out their God-given purpose.

Encourager

Holy Spirit, I ask that you help me encourage my husband. Please help me to speak life over his dreams, visions, and goals. Lord, I understand that being submitted to my man of valor is something only you can empower me to do. So Father, thank you for helping me see my husband the way you do and to speak life over him no matter our circumstances. Lord, I ask that you give me words like honey to heal in tough situations. (Proverbs 16:24)

LORD, I ask that you help me speak encouragement, life over my husband and the fruit of my womb. Lord, whether or not we have natural children, I ask for your grace to love, uplift and encourage those who come into our sphere of influence. Holy Spirit, please teach me to speak your Word in every season. Father, would you give me the spirit of gentleness when I speak? Jesus I ask that you would help me to adorn myself with a gentle and quiet spirit.

I want to be known as a woman after your own heart. Help me to show grace, love, honor and respect to your people and my husband. Thank you for teaching me through your word to use my mouth to create the realities of what I want to see. Lord, in times when I do not understand, help me to support the things that you support. Father, I desire to be the voice urging him to obey and follow you to the ends of the earth. Let my word not tear down. Allow me to find strength in the mystery. Allow my faith talk to stir his and let us come together to achieve all you have purposed for us to do.

Holy Standard

Lord, I thank you for giving us your standard. Jesus, I thank you for calling us to live worthy of the call you have placed on our lives. Lord, I ask that you help us both individually and collectively to run away from the standard of the world and run to the standard that you've set up for your people. Lord Jesus, let your Word be a lamp unto our feet and a light unto our path. God, we ask that all the things we do would be pleasing to you. Father, help us to hide your Word in our hearts so that we might not sin against you. Please help us to meditate on your Word day and night. Holy Spirit, draw us closer to you so that your leading becomes louder than the voice of the world. Father, help us to be in the world but not of it. I thank you that your Word is sure footing to stand on. I thank you that you are our strength, making our feet like a deer's feet to give us the ability to tread on high places. (Habakkuk 3:19) Lord, help us to be in the world but not of it. Permit us to minister your love to a lost and dying world without compromising your standards.

Honesty

Lord Jesus, thank you for being the way, the truth, and the life. God, I thank you that my spouse and I will share honest communication. Lord, I thank you that we will abide in your Word and truly follow you as your disciples. Lord, I thank you that we will know the truth, and the truth will set us free. Holy Spirit, I thank you for guiding us into all truth. Lord, help us to be steered by holiness not our flesh. We choose to die to our flesh and live to the Spirit of truth. Father, I thank you that you will remove deceit and lying from our spirit. Lord, we repent for the times we have lied or been deceitful. Lord, your Word says, "Truthful lips endure forever, but a lying tongue is but for a moment. Deceit is in the heart of those who devise evil, but those who plan peace have joy." Proverbs 12:19-20 ESV Lord, help us to plan peace so that we have joy. Lord, we know that your joy is our strength. God, we are so grateful for your incredible grace, and we ask that you continue to mold us and our heart's desire to yours.

Continue to Pursue

Father, thank you for pursuing me through the Holy Spirit. Lord, I thank you for the time I did not know you, that you protected me and called out to my spirit. Lord, I thank you for continuing to pursue your bride and the church. Thank you for the example you show us of the pursuit in the book of Hosea. Lord, I thank you that we cannot run from your love because you will seek us out. I thank you that there is no height nor depth, things done, or anything I can do to separate me from your love Jesus! As a husband, help me to love your daughter this way. Lord, you keep pursuing a relationship with me after I received salvation. You keep showing me new depths of you and myself. Please help me to give my best to my wife and family. Help me to prioritize my relationship with you, so the overflow is evident to my wife. Please help me to remember to cherish the wife of my youth/age as you have given her to me. Lord, help me to always be intoxicated in her love. Proverbs 5:19

Baggage

Father, in the name of Jesus, I ask that you break every unclean soul tie of my past and present. Father, I thank you that you have the ability and desire for me to walk in purity and freedom. Lord, I ask forgiveness for every misstep that caused me to take on a weight that was never mine to carry. Lord, your Word says, *"Take your yoke, and learn from you, for you are gentle and lowly in heart, and I will find rest for my soul. For your yoke is easy, and your burden is light."* Matthew 11:29-30 ESV (paraphrased), so I ask that you help me give you every burden and every bit of baggage I am holding on to.

Lord, I release it all to you. Lord, I release the shame, the guilt, and the embarrassment of my past. I release my inconsistency, pride, and independence to carry things I should not carry to you. Lord, would You help me to walk free, free in your presence, free in your love, and free in the love of my spouse. I give myself to you again. I thank you for showing me anything that I have held on to in the natural or the spirit that I need to release. Holy Spirit would you lead and guide me to remove anything in me that cannot go with me into this marriage. Father, I want to walk in freedom from anything that would hinder you getting the glory from our lives. Lord, I ask that you help me not pick up any weight but yours in Jesus' name. Amen

Relationship with Christ

Jesus, help me remember I've made a covenant with you. Lord, I know that being a part of your church means I am your bride. I have vowed myself to you **first**. Lord, I break every chain of idolatry tied to marriage or any other thing that I've allowed to come before you. Thank you for the privilege of showing your relationship to the church on Earth with my spouse. Please allow us to be a picture of your sacrificial love. Lord Jesus, help me to keep our relationship number one in my heart. I desire to spend time with you, maintaining constant communication (praying without ceasing) all the days of my life.

Holy Spirit, guide me to your feet daily. Lord, you commanded that we have no other gods before you, including my spouse, my children, or anything else that would put a wedge between us. Lord Jesus, I surrender to your will and ask that you keep my husband and I both close to your heart as we join in covenant. Help me honor you and let our love overflow to my spouse on Earth. I thank you for all these things in the name of Jesus, Amen.

Salvation

If you have made it this far in the book and realize that you have not truly made a commitment to Jesus. If you have not trusted Him with your soul, you can ask Him into your heart right now.

Jesus, I confess that you are Lord. I believe I have fallen short of your standard through sin. I know that I need redemption through your blood. I believe that you lived a sinless life and became the perfect sacrifice for my sins. Thank you for making a way to put me back in right standing with *our* Father. Lord, ask not only that you save me but that you would lead my life. I surrender my heart to you. Holy Spirit, I invite you to change me from the inside out so that I look more like Jesus each day. Thank you for saving me. I will follow you, in Jesus name, Amen.

Favor

Lord, I thank you that you are with me! I thank you for loving and seeing me. Father, I thank you for giving me your son for my freedom. Lord, who am I that you are mindful of me? I thank you that the veil was torn and that the blood covers me. I thank you for the access you give me. Thank you for allowing me access to the king of kings, the creator. Lord, I thank you for giving me access to you. I thank you for the favor you allow me as a believer and for the favor you placed on my life. Your Word says, "*For you bless the righteous, O Lord; you cover me with favor as with a* shield." Psalm 5:12 ESV. Lord, you bless the righteous, O Lord; you cover me with favor as with a shield." Psalm 5:12 ESV I am so grateful for your great and steadfast love towards me. Lord, you never fail; you work all things together for my good. (Husband: Lord, you promised: *"He who finds a wife finds a good thing and obtains favor from the Lord."* Proverbs 18:22 ESV Lord, I found my good thing, so I expect your favor. I thank you that I can come boldly to you because I am your child.)

Communication

Lord, thank you for clearing the lines for communication with you. Lord, I'm grateful I can always come to you with my heart, joy, sorrow, and fury. Lord, I thank you that I always have access to you. I thank you for honoring the way I communicate with you. Thank you for allowing me to communicate with you through dance, song, journaling, and the silence of my noisy heart. Father, I thank you for always being attentive to my voice and for ripping the veil when you died for my sins from top to bottom so I could sup with you.

Lord, thank you for helping me to pray without ceasing and for a listening heart. Lord, I ask that you help me not only to hear but to listen and obey. Lord, I thank you that our communication will allow me to communicate with my spouse. Lord, empower me to always speak tender words dripping with honey. God, your Word says that words with honey can heal, let me speak healing words. Lord, I thank you for the power of life and death being in my tongue.

I thank you that I will speak life over myself, my marriage, my spouse, my home, and my legacy. Lord Jesus, will you help me to come to you when I don't have the patience to speak patiently with those with whom you've blessed me. Lord, open my heart to hear you, to feel heard, and to hear my spouse. Lord, help me to always restore in a spirit of gentleness. Lord, help me always to believe the best and to be forgiving. I thank you for good success in communication. I thank you that speaking life will be the culture of our marriage. I thank you for honesty and honor in our relationship. In Jesus' name, Amen.

Scriptures

"Elijah was a man with a nature like ours, and he prayed fervently that it might not rain, and for three years and six months it did not rain on the Earth. Then he prayed again, and Heaven gave rain, and the Earth bore its fruit. My brothers, if anyone among you wanders from the truth and someone brings him back, let him know that whoever brings back a sinner from his wandering will save his soul from death and will cover a multitude of sins."
    James 5:17-20 ESV

"And when you fast, do not look gloomy like the hypocrites, for they disfigure their faces that their fasting may be seen by others. Truly, I say to you, they have received their reward. But when you fast, anoint your head and wash your face, that your fasting may not be seen by others but by your Father who is in secret. And your Father who sees in secret will reward you."
    Matthew 6:16-18 ESV

' Therefore a man shall leave his father and his mother and hold fast to his wife, and they shall become one flesh. And the man and his wife were both naked and were not ashamed.'
    Genesis 2:24-25 ESV

So Jesus said to them, "Because of your unbelief; for assuredly, I say to you, if you have faith as a mustard seed, you will say to this mountain, 'Move

from here to there,' and it will move, and nothing will be impossible for you. However, this kind does not go out except by prayer and fasting."
   Matthew 17:20-21 NKJV

'So you will find favor and good success in the sight of God and man. Trust in the Lord with all your heart, and do not lean on your own understanding. In all your ways acknowledge him, and he will make straight your paths. '
   Proverbs 3:4-6 ESV

'The Lord will hold you in his hand for all to see— a splendid crown in the hand of God. Never again will you be called "The Forsaken City" or "The Desolate Land." Your new name will be "The City of God's Delight" and "The Bride of God," for the Lord delights in you and will claim you as his bride. '
   Isaiah 62:3-4 NLT

'For the whole law is fulfilled in one word: "You shall love your neighbor as yourself." But the fruit of the Spirit is love, joy, peace, patience, kindness, goodness, faithfulness, gentleness, self-control; against such things there is no law. And those who belong to Christ Jesus have crucified the flesh with its passions and desires. If we live by the Spirit, let us also keep in step with the Spirit. '
   Galatians 5:14, 22-25 ESV

'But what does it say? "The word is near you, in your mouth and in your heart" (that is, the word of faith that we proclaim); because, if you confess with your mouth that Jesus is Lord and believe in your heart that God raised him from the dead, you will be saved. For with the heart one believes and is justified, and with the mouth one confesses and is saved. For the Scripture says, "Everyone who believes in him will not be put

to shame." For there is no distinction between Jew and Greek; for the same Lord is Lord of all, bestowing his riches on all who call on him. For "everyone who calls on the name of the Lord will be saved."'
   Romans 10:8-13 ESV

About the Author

Janiela Russell is a believer born and raised in metro Detroit. She accepted Jesus at the ripe old age of four and has been following him ever since. Janiela is passionate about people, faith and coffee shops. She is the founder of Noble Publishing House and currently resides in Tulsa, OK. Her desire is to equip people for healthy relationships especially in the context of marriage and friendship.

You can connect with me on:
- https://www.noblepublishinghouse.com
- https://www.facebook.com/janiela.russell
- https://www.instagram.com/janielarussell

www.ingramcontent.com/pod-product-compliance
Lightning Source LLC
Chambersburg PA
CBHW030454100526
44580CB00010B/125/J